D1256812

Distribution Channel Strategy for Export Marketing
The Case of Hong Kong Firms

Research for Business Decisions, No. 67

Richard N. Farmer, Series Editor

Professor of International Business
Indiana University

Other Titles in This Series

Distribution Channel Strategy for Export Marketing
The Case of Hong Kong Firms

by
T.S. Chan

UMI RESEARCH PRESS

Ann Arbor, Michigan

Produced and distributed by
UMI Research Press
an imprint of
University Microfilms International
Ann Arbor, Michigan 48106

Library of Congress Cataloging in Publication Data

Chan, Tsang-sing, 1950-
Distribution channel strategy for export
marketing.

(Research for business decisions ; no. 67)
Revision of thesis (D.B.A.)–Indiana University,
1981.
Bibliography: p.
Includes index.
1. Export marketing–Hong Kong. 2. Marketing
channels–Hong Kong. I. Title. II. Series.

HF1009.5.C45 1983   658.8'48'095125   83-18158
ISBN 0-8357-1494-2

To Amelia, Jamie, and Justin

Contents

Tables

Foreword

Although Hong Kong is a tiny British Colony with a population of over five million, it ranks among the top nations of the world in trading. Hong Kong's record of economic growth and development over the past two decades has resulted in Hong Kong's emergence to economic prominence. The unique nature of Hong Kong's economy makes Hong Kong an ideal location to study export marketing strategy.

To meet the challenge of overseas competition and surmount the growing threat of protectionism, Hong Kong manufacturers need to plan ahead for long-run survival. Refinement and modification of the export distribution channels are likely to play an increasingly important role in providing support for further growth and expansion.

The large body of literature in distribution channels is almost exclusively concerned with distribution channels in a domestic context, the domestic firms engaging in international operations through exporting is almost completely overlooked. Besides, no serious empirical research that studies Hong Kong's export distribution channels can be found. The purpose of this book is to gain insights into how Hong Kong managers devise strategies and make decisions for domestic manufacturing firms in export distribution channels. This book investigates the critical factors influencing Hong Kong manufacturers' formulation of export distribution channel strategies, focusing on their distribution channel evaluation and modification processes.

The book's findings reveal that formulation of export distribution channel strategy is closely related with consideration of company goals as well as important forces in the international environment. The firms' export goals often change toward expansion as the volume of exports increases. The change toward expansion in export goals tend to result in firms placing greater emphasis on distribution channel strategy. The Hong Kong manufacturing firms are absorbing export distribution channel functions from existing channel intermediaries as a response to higher levels of overseas competition and trade restrictions.

The findings indicate that firms which perform channel evaluation on a more frequent basis tend to be seeking greater control over their export distribution channels through a greater degree of involvement in the export channels. There exists a tendency among the participating firms to change their export channel structures toward more direct exporting and less delegating through indirect exporting.

Among the firms involved in the in-depth interview process, there is little evidence of any systematic development of strategic marketing planning. This book contains a sequential process for planning the export distribution channels. Consequently, this book can have important implications for business people engaging in or considering exporting to foreign markets. It is likely that this book will be of interest to government officials and policy makers in developing countries, especially those following an export-led industrialization growth path, as the information provided can be used to expand or amend existing programs in promoting exports.

Credit for assistance is owed to many. This book has profited greatly from the insightful comments and suggestions of: Richard N. Farmer, Indiana University; Kenneth Simmonds, London Business School; and K.C. Mun, The Chinese University of Hong Kong. I especially want to credit Joseph C. Miller of Indiana University for his contribution to the strategic planning portion of this book. To K.Y. Ho, I express my appreciation for his assistance in administering the questionnaire. My gratitude also extends to all the business executives who took time out of their busy schedules to participate in the questionnaire survey and the interview process.

While many persons have contributed positively to this book, I assume full responsibility for any errors or shortcomings and invite criticisms and suggestions from every reader.

T.S. Chan
Hong Kong

1

Introduction

The Problem

Export distribution of manufactured goods has played a key role in Hong Kong's economy. The degree to which Hong Kong relies on exports can be seen from the ratio between domestic exports and Gross Domestic Product (GDP). As a percentage of GDP, domestic exports constituted around 50 percent of GDP in the early 1960s. Between 1965 and 1970, the ratio increased to a peak of 71 percent. This ratio dropped to 60 percent in the recession year of 1975. From 1976 to 1982, domestic exports were around 65 percent of GDP.[1] There is no doubt that the export-oriented manufacturing industries are the backbone of the Hong Kong economy.

In selecting the export distribution channels or export channels of distribution for their products, the Hong Kong manufacturing firms may choose to have all or part of the channel functions performed by external agencies or may choose to perform all of the channel functions internally. The formulation of effective channel of distribution strategies that result in efficient flows of products from the producer in Hong Kong to customers in the foreign target market is one of the major problems of most Hong Kong manufacturing firms.

The dynamic nature of the international environment makes it necessary for the Hong Kong manufacturing firms to evaluate the performance of distribution channels on a regular basis. When there is deviation from expected performance levels, the management must evaluate different channel strategies and implement modification in the channel structure. Therefore, given the export distribution of the Hong Kong manufacturing firms and the international environment in which they operate, a study of how managers devise strategies and make decisions can provide valuable conclusions to the Hong Kong business community, as well as managers and policy makers in all developing countries that are following an export-led industrialization growth path.

Research Objectives and Questions

The specific objectives of the research are:

1. To identify the critical factors influencing the Hong Kong manufacturers' formulation of strategies in export channels.
2. To examine the processes of evaluation and modification in export distribution channels of the Hong Kong manufacturing firms.
3. To indicate whether and how the Hong Kong manufacturers can plan, organize, and control the export distribution channels.

The research attempts to answer such questions as:

1. How is the export distribution channel selected by the Hong Kong manufacturing firms? What factors affect the choice of an appropriate export distribution channel?
2. Do the manufacturing firms in Hong Kong make structural and operational modification in their export channel strategies to accommodate changes associated with expansion in export markets?
3. What specific criteria are used to evaluate the export distribution channel? How often is the export channel evaluated? Who is involved in the evaluation?

Hypotheses

Exploratory Proposition I: Most larger and more successful Hong Kong manufacturing firms formulate channel strategies for export distribution based upon company goals and major forces in the international environment.

   Hypothesis 1:   As the volume of exports increases, goals of the larger and more successful Hong Kong manufacturing firms will become more committed to expanding their export programs leading to greater emphasis on distribution channel strategy.

   Hypothesis 2:   The larger and more successful Hong Kong manufacturing firms will respond to increases in overseas competition and trade restrictions in importing countries by performing an increased proportion of channel functions, such as financing inventory, financing and developing promotional programs, and other service or financial functions for agencies or institutions in the existing export channel structures.

Exploratory Proposition II: Most larger and more successful Hong Kong manufacturing firms perform evaluation on a regular basis, and make modification in export distribution channels as a result of strategic marketing planning.

Hypothesis 3: Based upon evaluation conducted on a regular basis, the larger and more successful Hong Kong manufacturing firms will attempt to seek greater control over their export distribution channels by changing the export channel structures toward more direct exporting and less delegating through indirect exporting.

Definitions

a.*Export:* Export generally refers to movement of commodities or merchandise from one country to other countries in the world. For the purpose of this study, export refers to the movement of domestically manufactured commodities or merchandise from Hong Kong to other countries.

b. *Export Distribution Channel:* An organized network of agencies and institutions which perform all the activities required to move products from the producer in Hong Kong to customers in the foreign target markets.

c. *Channel Strategy:* In principle, strategy is the primary means of reaching basic goals and objectives of the firm. As related to export distribution, a channel strategy represents planning decisions and implementation of action on getting products to customers at desired foreign target market and at desired time.

d. *Direct Exporting:* Direct exporting results when the firm performs the bulk of the export channel functions itself through an export department, export manager, or sales subsidiaries in foreign target markets.

e. *Indirect Exporting:* Indirect exporting occurs when the firm's products are sold in foreign markets but no special activity for exporting is carried within the firm.

Discussion

The first exploratory proposition implies that most larger and more successful Hong Kong manufacturing firms are faced with a decision in formulating strategies for their export distribution channels. The manufacturing firms' selection of channel strategy is a function of company goals. For example, if a manufacturing firm has a new performance goal of achieving a higher average annual return, the distribution objective can be changed from selective market coverage to intensive market coverage leading to formulation of new channel strategies. The selection of channel strategy for export distribution is also affected by forces in the international environment. Because the distribution of products in foreign markets moves the manufacturers into the arena of international operations, the firms encounter a complex environment of cultural forces, economic forces, competition, and political and institutional conditions.

Hypothesis 1 deals with the issue of changes in company goals as the volume of export increases or when export activity becomes mature. Goals and objectives of export distribution channels will change to reflect changes in company goals. For example, with the higher export volume, there will be a tendency for the manufacturing firms interested in expanding their export programs to place greater emphasis on distribution channel strategy, such as control from higher levels of authority within the firms.

Hypothesis 2 suggests that the firms' channel strategy will be modified according to the direction and extent of changes of major forces in the complex international environment. The Hong Kong manufacturers can respond to a change in international environment by shifting functions to or from existing channel agencies or institutions. For example, in response to increased competition from South Korea and Taiwan, the Hong Kong manufacturing firms can affect their relationships with existing channel agencies or institutions by providing financial assistance in inventory, financing and developing promotional programs, or other service or financial incentives. The manufactuers are absorbing export channel functions from existing channel agencies or institutions by performing an increased proportion of the channel functions themselves.

The second exploratory proposition considers the integration of channel planning into the strategic planning for exports. Most firms can, but few have mastered strategic marketing planning. The larger and more successful Hong Kong manufacturing firms will formulate or modify its channel strategy for export distribution after careful development of strategic marketing plans.

Hypothesis 3 states that as a result of evaluation conducted on a regular basis, there will be a tendency for the larger and more successful Hong Kong manufacturing firms to change their export channel structures in an attempt to gain control over the distribution of their products. The channel structure will move from the use of external agencies or institutions towards internalized sales or marketing subsidiaries in the foreign target markets. Even though the manufacturers may continue to rely on channel agencies or institutions in foreign markets, they are in a stronger position to influence their performance because they may have subsidiaries operating in the same market.

Background and Significance of the Problem

Although Hong Kong is a tiny British colony with a population of 5.5 million, it ranks among the top nations of the world in trading. The composition of domestic exports is heavily weighed toward clothing and electronic products, which together comprised over 54 percent of total domestic exports in 1982.[2]

This proportion has been affected downwardly by the quotas and voluntary restraints on imports imposed on Hong Kong by the United States and the European Economic Community, which together absorbed 62 percent of Hong Kong's domestic exports.[3] To a large extent, worldwide economic conditions can adversely affect Hong Kong's manufacturing industries, because demand for Hong Kong products and changes in trade restrictions tend to be a function of the level of economic activity in importing countries.

Hong Kong has concentrated on labor intensive, low technology industries. In the '50s and '60s, these low capital, low skill export-oriented industries provided the economy of Hong Kong with rapid growth. However, since the end of the '60s, competitors in neighboring countries became a real threat to Hong Kong manufacturers. Several developing countries in Asia, such as South Korea, Taiwan, Singapore, Malaysia, the Philippines, and Indonesia, where workers are plentiful at low wages, are emulating Hong Kong's export-led growth strategy and following Hong Kong closely in its trails of success. With the rapidly increasing wages of Hong Kong workers, labor cost is no longer an advantage for Hong Kong manufacturers. The low wages in neighboring countries represent a disconcerting ability of foreign competitors to outprice Hong Kong manufacturers in the world market.

Partly due to the result of Hong Kong's trade growth and partly to the response of manufacturers to trade restrictions, some Hong Kong manufacturing firms have been gradually upgrading their products and increasing prices to match the higher quality. In this respect, Hong Kong is following the footsteps of Japan, which has completely overcome the image of low quality, low price products of imitations. Hong Kong is rapidly shedding the cheap product image that has been attached to its exports, and there is growing acceptance of the quality of higher priced Hong Kong products.

To meet the challenge of overseas competitors and overcome the threat of protectionism, it is necessary for Hong Kong manufacturers to plan ahead for the long-run and be prepared for any adverse economic changes. One alternative is to shift from producing labor intensive products to technology intensive products and to diversify into areas of more sophisticated products with higher added value for growth. While the philosophy of diversification is logically sound, most Hong Kong manufacturers seem to have little interest in pursuing in this direction. Hong Kong manufacturing industries rely heavily on initiative from individual manufacturers to prosper and grow, because the Hong Kong government supports the nonintervention policy of laissez faire. Government export subsidies are nonexistent in Hong Kong. This is why most manufacturers are unwilling to risk their investment in diversification without long-term cooperation and assistance from the government.

Another alternative is to develop effective channel strategy for export distribution. Export channel strategy is the area most likely to play an increasingly important role in Hong Kong manufacturers' growth and expansion. Increased emphasis on channel strategy is more important than any other alternative because a large proportion of the retail price is tied up in distribution. Moreover, refinement of export distribution channel can yield lower costs and higher profits.

Effective channel strategy for export distribution is important for several reasons: (1) it determines how and where the product will be made available in the world market; (2) the choice of a channel structure is closely interrelated with other variables in the export marketing mix, such as product, price, and promotion. If the manufacturers' products do not reach target customers in the foreign markets, all other marketing efforts are wasted. This fact also implies the importance of channel strategy in the attainment of strategic objectives in export operations. Therefore, any study that will contribute in helping managers to understand and optimize channel strategy formulation in export distribution will be of significant value to Hong Kong manufacturers.

The primary contribution of this research will be the insight provided by its empirical nature, since research of this type has been absent from the channels literature. Most of the literature in channels addresses distribution channels in the domestic context. The few pieces of literature in international distrubution channels have been directed mainly toward multinational firms which often have different motives for entering international distribution. The domestic firms which enter international distribution through exporting, such as most Hong Kong manufacturing firms, have been overlooked with regard to the application of channel concepts in export distribution.

Since only larger and more successful Hong Kong manufacturing firms in clothing and electronics were included in the sample, the results of this study will benefit those less successful firms in Hong Kong as well as those presently considering exporting to foreign markets.

The findings of this study can have important implications for business managers, as well as government officials and policy makers in other developing countries, especially those that are following an export-led industrialization growth path. Such information can help managers in these developing countries to formulate effective channel strategy. Policy makers in developing countries who are responsible for stimulating exports can use the information to expand or amend existing government programs in promoting exports.

Finally, it is hoped that the idea and findings of this book will induce other researchers to pursue some of the questions involved in the area of export distribution channels.

Literature Review

Distribution channel is the managerial battlefield in which the marketing strategy of each business firm either succeeds or fails. During recent years, distribution strategy has been gaining more importance, mainly due to the large proportion of distribution factor in the retail price and the increasing higher transportation costs (Lusch, et al., 1976).

Studies of distribution channels may be classified in two ways. Some are managerial, oriented to the perspective of the individual firm. This book falls into this category. They determine the types of relationship the firm must establish with other agencies or institutions to market a product. The second type of study looks at the character of the distribution channel as a whole. The purpose of such study is to identify and to explain the basis for group of firms that make up the channel (Bucklin, 1966).

The large body of literature in distribution channels addresses channels in a domestic context. The manager responsible for channel strategy must design and select the appropriate channel system that will maximize profits and reduce costs. The manager must analyze and understand the rationale of channel design and the nature of changing channel structure (Kollat, et al., 1972). Therefore, the manager must study the following factors carefully in order to develop viable channel relationships: (1) selected target market; (2) the rest of the marketing mix; (3) company resources; (4) competition and other external forces; and (5) current and anticipated distribution structure in the product industry (Mallen, 1972).

Marketing theorists often disagree on the explanation and determination of channel structure. The channel structure has been viewed as a function of product life cycle, physical distribution systems and effective communication networks (Michman, 1971). However, Weigand has suggested a direct relationship between the size and the type of distribution channel structure used, with large firms being more likely to adopt vertical integration (Weigand, 1963). The most detailed theory of distribution channel structure was developed by Bucklin in 1966. This theory is based on the premise that the fundamental activities involved in distribution channels are largely in the twin flow of product and title. Given the demand of consumers, the inherent cost structure of performing different tasks, and a reasonably perfect market structure, outputs, functions, and institutions become arranged into a channel structure (Bucklin, 1966). Bucklin's theory of channel structure is based on the postponement and speculation concept (Bucklin, 1965). The concept of postponement suggests that marketing costs can be reduced by postponement of changes in the form and identity of a product and the inventory location. The demand of a product is more easily forecasted the closer to the time of purchase, postponement can reduce costs by cutting down uncertainty costs and risk. Speculation is the opposite of postponement. The principle of speculation holds that changes in form, and the movement of goods to forward inventories, should be made as soon as possible to reduce the costs of the marketing system.

Management must select the most effective and efficient way for products to reach target customers in the market. The manager can initially adopt a preferred channel from available channel alternatives. As a result of evaluation, channel modification may occur to reflect the changes in customer needs and market conditions. When no alternative previously existed, management must design or develop new institutions or use existing institutions in a new way (Walters, 1977).

The appraisal process of channel performance must be related to the objective of the firm and must measure how well the channel meets the objectives. Revzan discusses various objectives of channel participants and then goes on to look at management tools used in the appraisal process. From the manufacturer's point of view, the major objectives in evaluating channel performance are: (1) to determine the importance of distribution channels in the company's overall marketing program; (2) to determine the direct and indirect relationship between alternative channels and the company's product offerings; (3) to determine the contribution of alternative channels to customer recognition, cost-profit position of the company, and the company's complete knowledge of market information. Basic tools appropriate for evaluating channel effectiveness include comparative sales analysis, distribution cost analysis, and various types of marketing research (Revzan, 1961).

Increased competition in international markets has led firms to place greater importance and attention on the distribution channel as the key variable in the marketing effort (Slijper, 1978). Several pieces of literature have attempted to discuss distribution channels in an international context (Keegan, 1972 and 1974; Sethe and Seth, 1973). These works have been directed toward the multinational firm. This is the opposite from the purely domestic firm which the great body of literature in channels addresses. The domestic firm engaging in international operations through exporting falls into neither of these categories.

Most texts in international marketing that discuss distribution channels in exporting tend to be prescriptive in nature (Kahler and Kramer, 1977; Terpstra, 1978). While there are occasional comments about export channel practices, many are usually based on the experience of the authors or the expectation that managers act rationally.

A search of the literature indicates that no serious empirical research has been done to study Hong Kong's export distribution channels. Domestic exports of Hong Kong have been well studied from a macro-economic point of view, as evidenced by the availability of many excellent studies (Jao, 1974; Hsia, et al., 1975; Lin and Ho, 1979). However, there is a lack of managerial and marketing orientation, and the treatment tends to be theoretical in nature. Most of the writings about Hong Kong's export marketing appear in trade journals or newsletters and deal with success stories or day-to-day problems of particular firms.

Searching beyond the Hong Kong scene reveals several empirical studies in export marketing. Two studies look at export management in the British engineering industry (Hunt, et al., 1967; Hunt, 1969). The first study revealed the export marketing policies of firms and identifies several factors affecting the individual firm's export effort and success. In the second study, weaknesses in managing export operations were discussed. Another study looks at an empirical framework of selecting overseas distributors for exports, the findings suggested several factors the exporter must consider in determining distributor attributes and the resulting structure (Ross, 1972). In a cross-sectional study of exporting firms, a variety of exporting methods were found (Tookey, Lea and McDougall, 1967). A study of 48 award-winning companies in the United Kingdom found that usage of overseas distributors was correlated with age of firm (Cunningham and Spigel, 1971). Looking at four Swedish exporting companies, agents were frequently used during the initial stage of internationalization of the firm (Johanson and Wiedersheim-Paul, 1975). In addition, a Canadian study of managerial export orientation focused on experiences, views, and attitudes of seniors managers in Canadian industries toward exporting, as well as the problems and rewards they perceive from this activity (Abdel-Malek, 1974). All of these empirical studies share one similarity: they utilized interviews or questionnaires (or a combination of the two methods) as the method of data collection.

Evidently, more empirical work is needed to improve the understanding of export distribution channels, especially those related to Hong Kong's export-oriented manufacturing firms. In addition, channel concepts developed for domestic firms can be applied to test the validity of their application in export channels of distribution. This book represents an attempt to meet these goals by gathering and analyzing data which depict an empirical profile of export channels of distribution of Hong Kong manufacturing firms in clothing and electronics industries.

Organization of the Study

Increased competition in international markets and the threat of protectionism have compelled Hong Kong manufacturing firms to place great importance toward distribution channels. The formulation of effective strategy and sound decision making in the export distribution channel are vital to the continuing success of Hong Kong manufacturers in foreign markets.

The remainder of this research is presented in chapters 2 through 5. Chapter 2 presents the historical background of industry and trade in Hong Kong. Hong Kong's manufacturing industry is described, special consideration is given to economic policy of Hong Kong government, and the chapter concludes with an examination of Hong Kong's external trade.

Chapter 3 deals with the research methodology. In this chapter, the research design and the field research are developed, topics discussed include research population and sample, pretesting, questionnaire administration, and interview procedure. The final part of this chapter explains possible limitations in drawing conclusions and making generalizations from the findings of this research.

The findings and discussion are presented in chapter 4. The first part examines the historical perspectives of clothing and electronics industries in Hong Kong. It follows with a look at how the two industries view various issues in export distribution channels and the extent and significance of differences among them. The final part of this chapter explores the relationship between channel involvement, channel evaluation, and characteristics of the firm, namely size, ownership, export sales growth, export experience, and size of exports.

In chapter 5, the most important conclusions of this research are summarized, and their implications for business managers, academicians and government officials are discussed. A sequential process for planning the export distribution channel is also explained. Finally, suggestions for future research are included.

2

Industry and Trade in Hong Kong

Hong Kong is a British Crown colony located in the southeastern coast of the People's Republic of China. It is comprised of Hong Kong Island, the Kowloon Peninsula, and the New Territories. Hong Kong Island and the Kowloon Peninsula were ceded by China to the British in 1841 and 1860 respectively. In 1898, the New Territories were leased to the British for a 99-year term.

Including the new reclamation, the total land area in Hong Kong is 403.75 square miles. Hong Kong has virtually no natural resources. Its one outstanding asset is the excellent, sheltered natural harbor. The colony depends heavily upon the export of domestically manufactured goods to pay for vital imports, including a major portion of its foods and raw materials.

Hong Kong is regarded as one of the few examples of a free enterprise economy in the world. It is gaining international reputation as a leading manufacturing and commercial center. Major factors contributing to this status include free enterprise and free trade policies, industrious workforce, sophisticated infrastructure, modern airport and seaport and excellent communication facilities.

Historical Background

Hong Kong was originally a trading center. It was declared a free port in 1841, and earned its income serving as an entrepot for British trade with southern China for the next 100 years. Although the economy included some manufacturing industries, their contribution to the total national income of Hong Kong was insignificant.

Hong Kong took a step forward in its industrial development in the early 1950s when two major events altered the emphasis of its economic structure. The change of government in China and the outbreak of the Korean War resulted in the United Nations's embargo on exports of strategic goods to China and the United States's restriction on any trade with China. With the loss of Chinese trade, Hong Kong was forced to find new ways of keeping its economy viable.

Hong Kong turned its labor skill and capital to domestic manufacturing for export markets. Factories were built, raw materials were imported and converted into finished goods. Manufacturing activities included textiles, foods and beverages, rubber and leather footwear, enamelware, and consumer goods like tooth brushes and fountain pens. Domestic exports rose from 15 percent of total exports in 1950 to around 70 percent in 1959, with the remainder consisting of reexports.[1]

In the early stages of Hong Kong's industrialization, a large proportion of the capital formation was from outside funds contributed by refugees and overseas Chinese. In late 1940s and 1950s, it was estimated that this source of funds amounted to HK\$ 300-600 million per annum.[2] Many Chinese industrialists moved their machinery and plants to Hong Kong, mainly because of political uncertainty in China. As a result of the Communist takeover in China, the flood of refugees entering Hong Kong created the valuable pool of cheap labor for manufacturing industries.

During the past two decades, Hong Kong has transformed from a trading port into an industrial center, with heavy emphasis on its manufacturing industry. Since 1950, Hong Kong has shown a capacity for growth and development that is unmatched by other developing countries of the world.

Manufacturing Industry in Hong Kong

The manufacturing industry in Hong Kong produces mainly light consumer goods. Key industries include clothing, electronics, plastic products, and textiles, which together account for about two-thirds of domestic exports and employ about the same proportion of the manufacturing workforce in 1982.[3] Only a small contribution comes from heavy industries such as machine tools and equipment, aircraft engineering, and ship building and repairing. The number of establishments and persons engaged, analyzed by manufacturing industry, can be found in table 2.1

Clothing manufacturing is the leading industry, accounting for over 35 percent of domestic exports and employing about 32 percent of Hong Kong's manufacturing workforce in 1982.[4] The clothing industry has grown from manufacturing basic items like underwear, shirt and gloves to leisure wear, outer garments, and high fashion dresses. It now produces high quality clothes and keeps abreast of the latest trends in fashion, two reasons why Hong Kong is the world's largest exporter of clothing.

In terms of export earnings, the second largest manufacturing industry is electronics. It employs about 10 percent of the manufacturing workforce and accounts for around 19 percent of domestic exports in 1982.[5] The industry has evolved from the assembly of simple transistor radios to the high quality and sophisticated products now being manufactured and exported. The range of products include transistor radios, computer memory systems, electronic calculators, transistors, television sets, integrated circuits, semi-conductors, television games, pre-packaged modules, and alarm systems.

The plastic industry, third in economic importance, has grown rapidly from its early production of mainly simple domestic wares and artificial flowers to the production of high quality toys and dolls, a wide variety of decorated articles, and household utensils. In fact, Hong Kong has become the world's largest exporter of plastic toys. In 1982, the plastic industry accounted for 9 percent of domestic exports and approximately 10 percent of the manufacturing workforce.[6]

The textile industry began with a few weaving and knitting establishments. In 1947, cotton spinning mills were set up when several Shanghai industrialists moved their capital and expertise to Hong Kong because of political upheavals in China. Since then the industry has been growing both vertically and horizontally—vertically from cotton spinning and weaving to dyeing and bleaching, stencilling and printing; horizontally from cotton to wool, silk and manmade fibers, from common printed fabrics to sophisticated printed fabrics.[7] The textile industry has been the keystone of Hong Kong industry. While most of its output is used by local manufacturers, it still accounted for 6 percent of domestic exports and employed 10 percent of the manufacturing workforce in 1982.[8]

The watch and clock industry has expanded rapidly in recent years. In 1982, it accounted for 9 percent of domestic exports and employed about 5 percent of the manufacturing workforce.[9] It produces a wide variety of watches and clocks, both electronic and mechanical, and quality watch components and accessories.

Other key light industries in Hong Kong include electrical machinery, apparatus and appliances, travel goods, handbags and similar articles, jewelry, footwear, and furniture and fixtures. Each of these industries produces a wide range and variety of products primarily for export markets.

Ship building and repairing industry has been the leading heavy industry in Hong Kong. The ship repairing sector provides excellent service at very reasonable cost, attracting numerous ship owners to bring their vessels to Hong Kong for repairs, overhauls, and conversions. The major ship building docks are capable of handling ships of up to 36,000 tons or about 210 meters in length.[10] The manufacture of machine tools and equipment provides mainly for the local industries. Major output includes mouldings, presses, shapers, drills, knitting machines, and electroplating equipment. The aircraft engineering industry enjoys international reputation for providing service and maintenance for the majority of airlines operating in Asia.

Economic Policy of Hong Kong Government

The government's principal role in the Hong Kong economy is to maintain a stable and steady framework for efficient and effective commercial and industrial operations. Apart from ensuring the provision of the infrastructure, the government exercises very little interference in the economy. The government adopts the laissez faire policy, which states that nonintervention is the best policy for creating a favorable climate for economic growth and development.

The government neither subsidizes domestic exports, nor protects the domestic market for Hong Kong manufacturers. In general, the government follows the following economic policies:[11]

1. *Low Taxation:* The government assesses low taxes for both personal and corporate incomes; the tax rates are 15 percent on individuals and partnerships, and 17 percent on corporations. The reasoning is that low taxation is conducive to domestic capital accumulation and tends to attract foreign investment.

2. *Surplus-prone Budget:* The government always seeks a balanced or surplus-prone budget to avoid public borrowing in the domestic and international capital market. The key objective is to maintain stability in the money and foreign exchange markets.

3. *Free Trade:* Hong Kong has always been a free port, with tariffs imposed only on tobacco, alcoholic liquors, and petroleum. The government believes that free trade is the best policy for an isolated city with few resources, as the absence of tariffs on imported materials and foodstuffs minimizes production costs and enables Hong Kong products to be more competitive in the world market. Besides, free trade can avoid the problem of misallocation of resources under protectionism.

4. *Unrestricted Movement of Money and Capital:* In order to attract capital investment from overseas, both real and financial, there is no exchange control or restriction on remittances of profit or capital overseas. As a result, Hong Kong has gained international reputation as a financial center, with a wide spectrum of financial institutions and expertise. It also draws a large proportion of the short- and long-term money from Asian investors. Appendix I provides a description of Hong Kong as a financial center.

5. *The 100 Percent Reserve Backing Monetary System:* The Hong Kong dollar is issued by private banks against 100 percent reserve backing of foreign exchange. The reserve backing is a major source of confidence in Hong Kong dollar, helping to draw capital inflow and foreign investment. A detailed description of the exchange value of the Hong Kong dollar can be found in Appendix II.

The Trade, Industry and Custom Department of Hong Kong government conducts external commercial relations within the framework of free trade policy. Hong Kong practices the rules of the General Agreement on Tariffs and Trade, the most prominent ones are restraints on textile exports to most major trading partners. A description of Hong Kong's international commerical relations is included in Appendix III.

In short, the economic policies of the Hong Kong government are stable and are based upon the philosophy of laissez faire, which encourages personal and corporate initiatives as well as investment. The corporate and personal taxation is low, the government maintains prudent fiscal policies, no exchange control or restriction on remittances, and the local currency is backed 100 percent by reserves.

External Trade

Hong Kong exports its manufactured foods in exchange for imports of foods, consumer foods, raw materials, and capital goods. Table 2.2 contains summary statistics of Hong Kong's external trade between 1977 and 1982. Total merchandise trade in 1982 amounted to HK$ 270,278 million, an increase of 4 percent from HK$ 260,537 million in 1981.[12] Total merchandise trade averaged about 22 percent increase per annum during this six-year period.

Exports

Domestic exports consist almost entirely of manufactured goods as shown in table 2.3. In 1982, clothing remained the leading manufacturing industry, exporting a total value of HK$ 28,824 million. Although the total value of clothing exports has been increasing over the years, the share of the domestic exports is decreasing gradually. The 34 percent share of domestic exports in 1982 represented a continuous decline from the 35 percent enjoyed by the clothing industry in 1981.

Domestic exports of electronic products continue to strengthen as the second largest export earner with a total value of HK$ 15,986 million in 1982, comparing to HK$ 15,774 million in 1981. Photographic and optical goods, and watches and clocks accounted for a total value of HK$ 8,148 million. Miscellaneous manufactured goods such as plastic toys and dolls, jewelry, goldsmith's and silversmith's wares, and other plastic articles were valued at HK$ 15,589 million. Other light manufactured articles such as textiles, electrical machinery, apparatus and appliances, travel goods, handbags and similar articles, footwear, machinery (other than electrical and electronic), printed matter, and furnitures and fixtures were also important exports.

The level of Hong Kong's export trade is determined by economic conditions and commercial policies in its overseas markets. In 1982, Hong Kong's top six markets, the United States, West Germany, China, Japan, and Australia, accounted for two-thirds of domestic exports of Hong Kong. The

United States alone absorbed 38 percent of the total, ranking as the leading market for Hong Kong. China overtook Japan to become Hong Kong's fourth largest export market, because of the various trade arrangements between China and businessmen in Hong Kong. Appendix IV discusses briefly Hong Kong's economic relations with China. Table 2.4 lists domestic exports of Hong Kong by countries between 1977 and 1982. Domestic exports are forecasted to grow at a positive rate of 5 percent in 1983, with the expected recovery largely in the second half of the year. [13]

Imports

Hong Kong is heavily dependent on imported resources which include raw materials and semi-processed goods, consumer products, and capital goods. Table 2.5 shows the imports of Hong Kong by principal commodities from 1980 to 1982.

In 1982, the HK$ 56,444 million imports of raw materials and semi-processed goods represented 40 percent of the year's total imports. The main items imported were fabrics of manmade fibers, iron and steel, raw cotton, watch and clock movements, woven cotton fabrics, plastic moulding materials, and transistors, diodes and circuits. The principal consumer products imported included diamonds, watches, radios, television sets, records, tape recorders and jewelry. The total value of HK$ 38,614 million of consumer goods represented 27 percent of total imports. Imports of capital goods were valued at HK$ 19,943 million or 14 percent of total imports, including electronic components and parts for machines, industrial machinery, office machines, and transport equipment. Imported foodstuffs consisted mainly of items such as fish, meat, fruits, and vegetables, amounting to HK$ 16,785 million or 12 percent of total imports.

China, Japan, and the United States were the three major suppliers of imports. In 1982, these three countries supplied 58 percent of all Hong Kong imports. Other important sources of imports were Taiwan, Singapore, United Kingdom, and South Korea. Among these countries, only imports from China and the United States recorded increases of 12 percent and 7 percent respectively. Another notable feature of 1982 was that China overtook Japan to become the largest supplier of Hong Kong imports. Table 2.6 presents imports of Hong Kong by countries from 1977 to 1982. In 1983, the import growth rate is expected to be around 7 percent in real terms. [14]

Re-exports

Re-exports have been a leading contribution to Hong Kong's positive export performance in recent years. In 1982, re-exports accounted for 35 percent of Hong Kong's total exports. The principal commodities re-exported were textiles and clothing, watches and clocks, machinery and transport equipment, telecommunication and sound recording apparatus and equipment, electrical machinery and appliances, and pharmaceutical products. Re-exports of Hong Kong by principal commodities from 1980 to 1982 are shown in table 2.7.

In 1982, the main countries of origin of the re-exports were China, Japan, and the United States. Hong Kong's entrepot role has been expanding, largely a reflection of China's more open trade policy and that country's position as the largest source of transshipments with the rest of the world. China became the largest re-export market in 1982, from sixteenth position in 1978. Other major re-export markets included the United States, Indonesia, Singapore, Taiwan, and Japan. Table 2.8 summaries re-exports of Hong Kong by countries of destination between 1977 and 1982. The mild worldwide recovery expected in 1983 should stimulate re-exports, particularly in respect with trade within the Southeast Asian region. The forecasted growth rate of re-exports in real terms is 12 percent.[15]

Balance of Trade

Hong Kong has not had a trade surplus in over 20 years.[16] It is important to find out whether the trade deficit is due to expansion and growth in manufacturing industries or simply to increased consumption of imported consumer goods. Looking back at table 2.2, the external trade of Hong Kong between 1977 and 1982, the trade deficit of HK$ 3,868 million created great concern among government economists in Hong Kong. A large part of the increase in trade deficit was attributed to imported consumer goods for final consumption, rather than materials for export manufacturing industries.[17]

The trade deficit of HK$ 9,148 in 1978 caused even more concern, especially because of the weakening effect upon the Hong Kong dollar. The trade deficit reached new levels of HK$ 13,408 million, HK$ 16,213 million, and HK$ 15,508 million in 1980, 1981, and 1982 respectively. However, there has been a slight improvement of the import contents when comparing the imports in 1977 and 1978. A greater proportion of the increase in imports was input for the export manufacturing sector. Incidentally, the larger deficits of 1980 through 1982 reflected the higher oil prices due to the Organization of Petroleum Exporting Countries' (OPEC) second round of oil price hikes.

The trade deficit has been financed over the years from two different sources. The amount of money flows to Hong Kong as capital investment, both financial and real, helping to provide positive foreign exchange balances.[18] Appendix V gives a brief description of direct foreign investments in Hong Kong. In addition, tourism is major source of foreign exchange. In 1982, there were over 2.6 million tourists, spending an estimated HK$ 8,900 million on goods and services while visiting Hong Kong.[19]

Summary

Hong Kong was originally an entrepot serving British trade with southern China. The outbreak of the Korean War and the subsequent United Nations's embargo on trade with China forced Hong Kong to transform its economy to domestic manufacturing for exporting. Since 1950, the growth and development in Hong Kong has been unmatched by other developing countries of the world.

Most of the manufacturing industries in Hong Kong are engaged in the production of light consumer goods. Key sectors include clothing, electronics, plastic toys and dolls, and textiles. Heavy industries such as machine tools and equipment, ship building and repairing, and aircraft engineering contribute only a small fraction of manufacturing output.

The economic policies of Hong Kong government are stable, and are based upon a philosophy of minimum interference to encourage investment and initiatives from businessmen and corporations.

Hong Kong's total merchandise trade has been increasing rapidly, representing an average of 22 percent per annum during 1977 to 1982. Domestic exports have been increasing dramatically, while the entrepot trade is reemerging with the phenomenal rise in re-exports. Although the trade deficit continue to increase, the content of imports shows a favorable shift toward raw materials and semi-processed goods for export manufacturing industries.

3

Research Methodology

A research design depends on research purpose. As discussed earlier in chapter 1, the main purpose of this research is to gain new insights into how managers devise strategies and make decisions for domestic manufacturing firms in export distribution channels. Since empirical research of this type has been absent from the channel literature, the role of this study represents what Selltiz et al have characterized as "exploratory" or "formulative" research.[1]

An exploratory study aims "to gain familiarity with a phenomenon or to achieve new insights into it, often in order to formulate a more precise research problem or to develop hypotheses."[2] By definition, en exploratory study involves investigation of problems on which little formal knowledge is available. The research design for exploratory study must be characterized by flexibility and versatility, to permit considerations of different aspects of the problem area.

Several propositions and hypotheses were specified in this study, in addition to statistically testing these propositions and hypotheses for acceptance or rejection, heavy emphasis was also placed on achieving familiarity with the relationships between specific characteristics of the firm, strategic market planning, and channel strategy formulation for export distribution. While the statistical techniques used in this study were not highly rigorous, the nature and complexity of the problem as well as the scope of this study made it impractical to use other techniques.

The exploratory nature of this research, in terms of kind and amount of information desired, necessitated the use of a combination of questionnaire and in-depth inteview methods. Based on the information gathered from the literature review, a questionnaire was formulated and sent to knowledgeable executives of 200 domestic manufacturing firms in the two leading industries in Hong Kong, clothing and electronics. Together they comprised approximately one-half of Hong Kong's domestic exports in 1982. Personal interviews were also conducted with executives of ten firms to gain more in-depth knowledge of export operations, with the main emphasis on distribution channel strategy. The remainder of this chapter presents a detailed description of the research design.

Field Research

Population and Sample Determination

The population of this study is defined as those nonmultinational manufacturing firms in clothing and electronics located in Hong Kong. In order to exclude export transactions between parent and subsidiary of multinational firms which might have entirely different motives for export operations than those purely export oriented manufacturing firms, only nonmultinational firms are included in the population.

Firms selected for the questionnaire survey as well as the subsequent in-depth interview were chosen on the basis of several criteria. This research aimed to study only those larger and more successful manufacturing firms in Hong Kong. Therefore, only firms with gross export sales in excess of HK$ 5 million were selected. In addition, the number of employees had to exceed 100 for the firm to be included in the sample. The surveyed firms exhibited a wide range of gross export sales from slightly above HK$ 5 million to over HK$ 100 million. These firms also varied in terms of the number of employees, with a range of 100 to over 2,000 workers.

The sample firms for this study were selected from the Members' Directory of the Federation of Hong Kong Industries.[3] A total of 200 firms were included in the sample: 130 clothing manufacturing firms and 70 electronics manufacturing firms. Ten firms were selected from the respondents of the questionnaire for the in-depth interview, with six firms and four firms from the clothing and electronics industries respectively.

Pretesting

A pretest was conducted to test the questionnaire and interview guide against four nonsample Hong Kong manufacturing firms. First, pretesting provided the knowledge about the time required to answer the questionnaire and to obtain the necessary information in the interview process. Second, the pretest helped to understand the degree of difficulty and ambiguity of the questionnaire. Finally, pretesting also helped in sharpening open-ended questions for in-depth interview as well as clarifying terms and languages as most interviews were conducted in Chinese.[4]

An important part of pretesting involved interviews with experts from trade associations, government sponsored organizations and universities. These interviews provided comments regarding research instruments and information on structure, growth, and development in the two Hong Kong industries under investigation: clothing and electronic products. For example, interviews were conducted with the manager of the Hong Kong Management Association,[5] and several faculty members of the Faculty of Business Administration at The Chinese University of Hong Kong.

The pretest was conducted over a one week period during May 1981. It was learned that some minor changes would be necessary to facilitate the collection of data. In particular, Chinese translations for specific marketing terms used were included in the questionnaire to reduce the difficulties that managers might have in understanding the question asked. Also, the amount of time required per interview could be reduced substantially if the interviewer took only brief notes and prepared detailed interview reports immediately after the interview. It was felt that cutting the interview time from 45 minutes to 30 minutes enhanced management's approval to participate in the interviews. Taping of interview sessions as an alternative to note taking was dropped, as it was believed to inhibit desirable responses from managers.

Questionnaire Administration

The structured questionnaire was used to provide comparable response data for an analysis of export distribution channel in Hong Kong's clothing and electronics industries. The questionnaire focused on three basic groups of questions. The first group of questions was designed to obtain basic data about sample manufacturing firms and their export operations. The second group contained questions which were aimed to collect data about structure and modification processes in export distribution channels of sample firms. Finally, group three consisted of questions which were designed to solicit responses about channel selection and evaluation decisions. The complete questionnaire can be found in Appendix VI.

With the cooperation of the Department of Marketing and International Business at The Chinese University of Hong Kong, a cover letter from the department signed by the researcher was sent with each questionnaire. This letter explained the nature and purpose of the research, as well as assuring the strict confidentiality of the questionnaire materials. A copy of the cover letter is included in Appendix VII. A self-addressed, stamped return envelope was enclosed with each questionnaire to provide convenience for, and induce cooperation from, firms selected for the questionnaire survey.

As a result of pretesting, it was felt that the response rate would be improved if the questionnaire was sent to a specific individual within each sample firm. Therefore, the questionnaire was mailed to the export manager or the manager in charge of export activity in each sample manufacturing firm, who would be involved in day-to-day export operations. The Members' Directory of the Federation of Hong Kong provided names of officers and detailed addresses for all the 200 firms selected in the sample.

Each questionnaire sent was coded to assist in identifying nonrespondants, so that follow up calls would reach only those "no" response firms. The initial return after the first week was 40 out of the 200 sent, a response rate of 20 percent. However, the initial return included 8 totally or partially unanswered questionnaires, resulting in an initial usable response rate of 16 percent.

One week after the first mailing of the questionnaire, the first follow up calls were made through the use of telephone calls to "no" response firms. For those firms that replied they did not receive the questionnaire, address corrections were requested and additional questionnaires were sent. At the end of the second week after the first mailing, 10 more questionnaires were received. Since they were all usable, the usable response increased to 21 percent. At the same time, the second follow up calls were made, again only to those "no" response firms. Four additional questionnaires, all usable, were received after the second follow up calls. At the end of the fourth week after the first mailing of questionnaire, it was assumed that the remaining "no" response firms were unwilling to participate in this research project.

During the one month period after the first mailing of questionnaire, a total of 54 questionnaires were returned. Accounting for the eight totally or partially unanswered questionnaires, the total usable response rate was 23 percent. The 46 usable questionnaires were comprised of the returns from 32 clothing manufacturing firms and 14 electronics manufacturing firms. Table 3.1 shows the distribution of usable responses of the questionnaire by industry. The usable response rate of 23 percent is considered highly satisfactory, since responding to questionnaires has not been a widely acceptable practice among businessmen in Hong Kong. There is a high degree of concern over disclosure of company information among most businessmen in Hong Kong, who fear it may adversely affect the competitiveness of their firms.

Interview Procedure

The main purpose of the in-depth interview was aimed at asking chief executive officers or members of top management in each of the selected firms open ended questions without having to conform to a rigid structure. The chief executive officer or member of top management would be able to provide views of export operations from the top of the organizational structure, especially in areas of goals, objectives, and policies which might affect strategy and structure in the export distribution channel.

The 10 firms interviewed were chosen from the respondents of the questionnaire survey. The selection of firms was made on the basis of size of firm, ownership status, relative size of exports, degree of involvement in the export distribution channel, and different stages of development in export operations.

Each interviewee was asked to express his views and experience relating to strategy in export distribution channels. The in-depth interview emphasized questions that discovered information necessary for explaining underlying strategic and structural rationale. In addition, exploratory questions designed to draw out the logical causation among strategy and performance were also included. The in-depth interview also provided examples for illustration. A complete interview guide is included in Appendix VIII.

Initial contacts with firms selected for the interview were made by telephone. The purpose of the interview was explained, and an appointment for a field visit was arranged if the executive contacted showed an interest in participating. In some cases, participation was not forthcoming, thus additional firms were selected and contacted. A total of 15 firms were contacted before approval from 10 firms had been received. Two firms declined to be interviewed without explanation, and the responsible executives were away from Hong Kong for the other three firms. The 10 firms interviewed comprised of six clothing manufacturers and four electronics manufacturers. Table 3.2 shows the distribution of firms interviewed by industry.

The average interview took 30 minutes to complete, with a range of 45 minutes for the longest interview and 20 minutes for the shortest one. Information gathered through the in-depth interview was helpful and constructive. Most executives interviewed were extremely candid in their views and provided information otherwise unobtainable by using questionnaire alone.

Limitations

Because of the exploratory nature of this study, care must be taken in drawing conclusions and making generalization. Major limitations of this study include the nonrandom nature of the sample, the low response rate of the questionnaire, and the small number of in-depth interviews. These preclude the use of many sophisticated statistical techniques in the analysis of collected information. In addition, statistical tests of significance are not applicable to the qualitative responses from in-depth interviews, which constitute a key proportion of information collected for this study.

For this reason, conclusions drawn from the findings of this study are not intended to be definitive, but rather to stimulate insights into the research area of export distribution channels for more definitive studies in the future.

Summary

This exploratory study employed two research methods: the questionnaire survey and in-depth interview provided the framework for data collection. A search of the literature for information related to export distribution channels provided the background for formulating the questionnaire. The questionnaire was mailed, together with a cover letter and self-addressed, stamped return envelope, to 200 Hong Kong manufacturing firms which included 130 clothing manufacturers and 70 electronics manufacturers. These firms were selected from the Members' Directory of the Federation of Hong Kong Industries. The total response rate of 27 percent was comprised of 23 percent usable responses and 4 percent unusable responses. Ten in-depth interviews were conducted with selected respondents of the questionnaire survey.

Because of the exploratory nature of this study and the limitations of the information collected, caution should be taken when making conclusions and inferences from the research results. The following chapter presents the findings and discussion of the questionnaire survey and in-depth interviews.

Table 2.1 Number of Establishments and Employment in Selected Manufacturing Industries

Industry	Establishments			Persons engaged		
	Sep 1980	Sep 1981	Sep 1982	Sep 1980	Sep 1981	Sep 1982
Food						
Bakery products	579	502	496	6 649	6 125	6 692
Canning and preserving of fruits and vegetables	100	89	88	2 594	1 535	1 248
Beverage						
Soft drinks and carbonated waters	14	11	13	3 362	3 079	3 359
Textiles						
Bleaching and dyeing	314	283	319	12 010	11 966	13 196
Cotton knitting	341	356	343	4 621	5 027	4 967
Cotton spinning	41	46	44	16 381	11 126	9 681
Cotton weaving	439	377	354	21 764	19 927	15 939
Embroideries	252	345	290	2 747	3 961	2 949
Knitwear from yarn	1 314	1 439	1 621	34 893	43 228	39 826
Made-up textile goods, except weaving apparel	306	343	347	4 348	4 225	4 022
Other textile finishing	119	106	101	2 773	2 230	1 965
Textile stencilling and printing	205	174	204	2 821	2 451	2 322
Woollen knitting	643	491	413	6 962	5 029	4 557
Woollen spinning	20	15	14	1 793	1 439	942
Wearing apparel, except footwear						
Garments except knitwear from yarn	7 250	7 443	7 348	220 459	223 585	220 267
Gloves	460	416	379	11 121	9 429	7 606
Handbags	860	916	889	15 620	15 345	13 417

Source: *Hong Kong Annual Report 1983*, (Hong Kong: Government Printer, 1983)

Table 2.1 continued

Footwear, except rubber, plastic and wooden footwear						
Footwear, except rubber, plastic and wooden footwear	509	562	554	6 629	8 079	7 327
Wood and corks products, except furniture						
Rattan articles	255	246	208	2 005	1 695	1 394
Wooden articles	484	458	454	2 380	2 111	1 931
Furniture and fixtures, except primarily of metal						
Wooden furniture and fixtures	1 309	1 318	1 325	9 288	9 386	7 941
Paper and paper products						
Paper boxes	847	868	873	7 520	7 655	7 144
Printing, publishing and allied industries						
Job printing	1 994	2 141	2 247	17 743	18 590	18 302
Newspaper printing	41	40	40	4 201	4 904	4 989
Chemicals and chemical products						
Drugs and medicines	251	248	280	2 245	2 151	2 401
Rubber products						
Rubber footwear	172	178	143	3 059	2 702	1 882

Industry	Establishments			Persons engaged		
	Sep 1980	Sep 1981	Sep 1982	Sep 1980	Sep 1981	Sep 1982
Plastic products						
Plastic flowers and foliage	405	418	350	4 934	4 855	3 753
Plastic toys	1 634	1 665	1 735	45 417	45 268	43 511
Miscellaneous plastic products, except plastic flowers and foliage and plastic toys	2 777	2 972	3 019	35 963	39 024	35 779
Non-metallic mineral products, except products of petroleum and coal						
Glass and glass products	177	160	159	1 951	1 890	1 560
Basic metal industries						
Iron and steel basic industries	163	153	155	3 199	3 059	2 942
Fabricated metal products, except machinery and equipment						
Aluminium ware	101	102	96	3 919	3 230	2 827
Buffing and polishing and electro-plating	771	783	736	7 217	7 542	6 684
Hand tools and general hardware	1 567	1 318	1 084	10 023	8 297	7 171
Metal toys	263	275	287	6 171	6 855	5 310
Structural metal products	787	834	841	3 890	4 159	4 219
Torches, torch cases and parts, except torch bulbs	52	51	48	5 245	4 469	4 095
Wrist watch bands	455	517	449	8 826	8 643	7 056
Machinery, except electrical						
Special industrial machinery and equipment, except metal and wood working machinery)	695	672	656	5 016	4 989	4 509

Table 2.1 continued

Electrical machinery, apparatus, appliances and supplies						
Dry batteries	14	11	18	2 437	2 361	1 937
Electrical appliances and housewares	417	434	492	16 240	19 400	17 814
Electrical industrial machinery and apparatus	211	223	245	3 776	4 302	4 722
Electronics	1 197	1 150	1 305	88 883	89 455	85 946
Phonograph records and magnetic tapes for records	104	135	129	3 927	4 440	4 575
Torch and electric bulbs	147	153	153	2 954	2 966	2 569
Transport equipment						
Aircraft repairing	2	2	2	3 957	4 150	3 983
Ship building and repairing	113	113	98	7 851	8 156	10 262
Professional and scientific, measuring and controlling equipment, and photographic and optical goods						
Photographic and optical goods	148	170	160	7 720	7 788	6 327
Watches and clocks	1 054	1 296	1 361	40 628	40 362	38 358
Other manufacturing industries						
Artificial pearls and imitation jewellery	357	404	364	3 042	3 276	2 676
Jewellery and related articles	674	726	738	7 847	8 902	8 330
Toys other than plastic toys, metal toys and wooden toys	217	236	216	3 987	4 298	2 876
Wigs	31	37	34	481	510	399

Table 2.2: External Trade

Year	Imports	Domestic Exports	Re-exports	Total Trade	Trade Balance
1977	48,701	35,004	9,829	93,534	−3,868
1978	63,056	40,711	13,196	116,964	−9,148
1979	85,837	55,912	20,022	161,771	−9,903
1980	111,651	68,171	30,072	209,893	−13,408
1981	138,375	80,423	41,739	260,537	−16,213
1982	142,893	83,032	44,353	270,278	−15,508

Value: HK$ Million

Source: *Hong Kong Trade Statistics,* various issues, (Hong Kong: Government Printer, 1978-83)

Table 2.3: Domestic Exports by Principal Commodities

Domestic exports

Section/division	1980	1981	HK$ Million 1982
Food and live animals chiefly for food			
Fish, crustacea and molluscs and preparations thereof	346	442	498
Vegetables and fruit	164	209	148
Miscellaneous edible products and preparations	180	227	286
Others	122	140	218
Sub-total	**813**	**1,018**	**1,150**
Beverages and tobacco			
Beverages	11	29	37
Tobacco and tobacco manufactures	103	162	154
Sub-total	**114**	**191**	**191**
Crude materials, inedible, except fuels			
Pulp and waste paper	157	138	129
Metalliferous ores and metal scrap	762	618	487
Crude animal and vegetable materials, n e s	119	154	134
Others	69	75	85
Sub-total	**1,108**	**985**	**835**
Mineral fuels, lubricants and related materials	**89**	**99**	**107**
Animal and vegetable oils, fats and waxes	**10**	**8**	**8**
Chemicals and related products, n e s			
Medicinal and pharmaceutical products	113	133	147
Essential oils and perfume materials: toilet, polishing and cleansing preparations	182	217	243
Artificial resins and plastic materials, and cellulose esters and ethers	123	221	210
Others	124	185	184
Sub-total	**542**	**755**	**785**

Manufactured goods classified chiefly by material			
Paper, paperboard and articles of paper pulp, of paper or of paperboard	209	221	259
Textile yarn, fabrics, made-up articles, n e s and related products	4,535	5,302	5,052
Non-metallic mineral manufactures, n e s	472	508	426
Manufactures of metal, n e s	2,037	2,027	2,044
Others	479	547	532
Sub-total	**7,732**	**8,606**	**8,313**
Machinery and transport equipment			
Telecommunications and sound recording and reproducing apparatus and equipment	5,030	5,618	5,672
Electrical machinery, apparatus and appliances, n e s, and electrical parts thereof	4,490	5,812	6,055
Others	2,856	3,613	3,347
Sub-total	**12,375**	**15,043**	**15,074**
Miscellaneous manufactured articles			
Sanitary, plumbing, heating and lighting fixtures and fittings, n e s	746	751	692
Furniture and parts thereof	386	389	335
Travel goods, handbags and similar containers	1,505	1,629	1,541
Articles of apparel and clothing accessories	23,258	28,288	28,824
Footwear	624	833	745
Photographic apparatus, equipment and supplies and optical goods, n e s; watches and clocks	7,119	8,101	8,148
Miscellaneous manufactured articles, n e s	11,020	13,235	15,589
Others	156	155	123
Sub-total	**44,814**	**53,381**	**55,996**
Commodities and transactions not classified according to kind	**574**	**338**	**574**
Total merchandise	**68,171**	**80,423**	**83,032**
Gold and specie	—	—	—
Grand total	**68,171**	**80,423**	**83,032**

Note: n e s = not elsewhere specified.

Source: *Hong Kong Annual Report 1983*, (Hong Kong: Government Printer, 1983)

Table 2.4: Domestic Exports by Countries

Domestic Exports	1977		1978		1979	
Destination	$	%	$	%	$	%
United States	13,552	38.7	15,125	37.2	18,797	33.6
Germany, Federal Republic	3,669	10.5	4,426	10.9	6,344	11.3
Britain	3,035	8.7	3,871	9.5	5,974	10.7
Japan	1,386	4.0	1,856	4.6	2,656	4.8
Australia	1,247	3.6	1,494	3.7	1,789	3.2
Canada	1,171	3.3	1,271	3.1	1,637	2.9
Singapore	904	2.6	1,104	2.7	1,413	2.5
Netherlands	763	2.2	937	2.3	1,406	2.5
France	472	1.3	575	1.4	1,004	1.8
Switzerland and Liechtenstein	572	1.6	683	1.7	949	1.7
Others	8,233	23.5	9,370	23.0	13,942	24.9
Merchandise total	**35,004**	**100.0**	**40,711**	**100.0**	**55,912**	**100.0**

Destination	1980 $	%	1981 $	%	1982 $	%
United States	22,591	33.1	29,200	36.3	31,223	37.6
United Kingdom	6,791	10.0	7,710	9.6	7,187	8.7
Germany, Federal Republic	7,384	10.8	7,048	8.8	7,031	8.5
China	1,605	2.4	2,924	3.6	3,806	4.6
Japan	2,329	3.4	2,940	3.7	3,167	3.8
Australia	1,941	2.8	2,710	3.4	2,832	3.4
Canada	1,782	2.6	2,355	2.9	2,637	3.2
Singapore	1,791	2.6	1,732	2.2	1,964	2.4
Netherlands	1,575	2.3	1,598	2.0	1,692	2.0
France	1,407	2.1	1,483	1.8	1,507	1.8
Others	18,975	27.8	20,724	25.8	19,985	24.1
Merchandise total	68,171	100.0	80,423	100.0	83,032	100.0

Value: HK$ Million

Source: *Hong Kong Trade Statistics*, various years, (Hong Kong: Government Printer, 1977-83)

Imports

Table 2.5: Imports by Principal Commodities

Section division	1980	1981	$ Million 1982
Dead and live animals chiefly for food			
live animals chiefly for food	1,635	1,897	2,097
Meat and meat preparations	1,475	1,631	2,024
Fish crustacea and molluscs and preparations thereof	1,776	2,007	2,767
Cereals and cereal preparations	1,556	1,893	1,874
Vegetables and fruit	2,843	3,705	4,158
Others	2,273	2,859	3,253
Sub-total	11,558	13,993	16,172
Beverages and tobacco			
Beverages	841	950	1,059
Tobacco and tobacco manufactures	743	1,109	1,268
Sub-total	1,583	2,060	2,327
Crude materials, inedible, except fuels			
Cork and wood	504	477	553
Textile fibres (other than wool tops) and their wastes (not manufactured into yarn or fabrics)	2,371	2,319	1,900
Crude animal and vegetable materials, n e s	1,671	1,680	2,034
Other	721	1,141	1,094
Sub-total	5,267	5,616	5,581
Fuels, lubricants and related materials			
Petroleum, petroleum products and related materials	7,642	10,646	10,609
Others	240	319	869
Sub-total	7,882	10,966	11,477
Animal and vegetable oils, fats and waxes			
vegetable oils and fats	368	414	389
Others	8	12	47
Sub-total	376	427	436

Dying tanning and colouring materials	960	1,154	1,299
Medicinal and pharmaceutical products	1,064	1,267	1,378
Resins and plastic materials, and cellulose esters and ethers	2,605	2,705	2,660
Other	3,305	3,934	4,150
Sub-total	7,934	9,059	9,486
Goods classified chiefly by material			
Fabrics, made-up articles, n e s, and related products	14,895	19,335	18,180
Non-metallic mineral manufactures, n e s	6,963	7,009	7,119
Iron and steel	3,426	3,842	4,035
Manufacturers of metal, n e s	2,272	2,833	3,125
Other	6,164	7,130	7,275
Sub-total	33,720	40,149	39,734
Machinery and transport equipment			
Telecommunications and sound recording and reproducing apparatus and equipment	4,471	6,122	4,899
Machinery, apparatus and appliances, n e s, and electrical parts thereof	7,526	9,931	10,442
Vehicles (including air-cushion vehicles)	3,311	4,398	3,574
Other	9,825	11,847	13,114
Sub-total	25,133	32,298	32,029
Miscellaneous manufactured articles			
Articles of apparel and clothing accessories	3,467	5,226	6,464
	631	839	1,063
Photographic apparatus, equipment and supplies and optical goods, n e s; watches and clocks	7,647	9,503	8,368
Miscellaneous manufactured articles, n e s	4,174	5,338	6,298
Other	1,708	2,273	2,786
Sub-total	17,628	23,179	24,978
Commodities and transactions not classified according to kind	569	628	671
merchandise	111,651	138,375	142,893
Species	2,991	8,930	8,193
Grand total	114,641	147,305	151,086

Note: n e s = not elsewhere specified

Source: *Hong Kong Annual Report 1983*, (Hong Kong: Government Printer, 1983)

Imports

Table 2.6: Import Trade by Countries

Source	1977 $	1977 %	1978 $	1978 %	1979 $	1979 %
Japan	11,547	23.7	14,405	22.8	19,320	22.5
China	8,082	16.6	10,550	16.7	15,130	17.6
United States	6,093	12.5	7,519	11.9	10,365	12.1
Taiwan	3,254	6.7	4,257	6.8	6,035	7.0
Singapore	2,888	5.9	3,219	5.1	4,821	5.6
Britain	2,192	4.5	2,975	4.7	4,350	5.1
Germany, Federal Republic	1,463	3.0	2,072	3.3	2,775	3.2
Switzerland and Liechtenstein	1,292	2.7	2,115	3.4	2,592	3.0
Republic of Korea (South Korea)	1,682	3.5	1,793	2.8	2,529	2.9
Australia	956	2.0	1,274	2.0	1,579	1.8
Others	9,252	19.0	12,876	20.4	16,340	19.0
Merchandise total	48,701	100.0	63,056	100.0	85,837	100.0

Source	1980 $	1980 %	1981 $	1981 %	1982 $	1982 %
China	21,948	19.7	29,510	21.3	32,935	23.0
Japan	25,644	23.0	32,130	23.2	31,540	22.1
United States	13,210	11.8	14,442	10.4	15,459	10.8
Singapore	7,384	6.6	10,627	7.7	10,207	7.1
Taiwan	7,961	7.1	10,762	7.8	10,198	7.1
United Kingdom	5,456	4.9	6,283	4.5	6,892	4.8
Republic of Korea (South Korea)	3,869	3.5	5,495	4.0	4,557	3.2
Germany, Federal Republic	2,883	2.6	3,383	2.4	3,506	2.5
Switzerland	2,897	2.6	2,848	2.1	2,669	1.9
Australia	1,698	1.5	2,005	1.4	2,266	1.6
Others	18,701	16.7	20,891	15.1	22,664	15.9
Merchandise total	111,651	100.0	138,375	100.0	142,893	100.0

Source: *Hong Kong Trade Statistics*, various years, (Hong Kong: Government Printer, 1977-83)

Table 2.7: Re-exports by Principal Commodities

Re-exports

Section/division	1980	1981	$ Million 1982
Food and live animals chiefly for food			
Fish, crustacea and molluscs and preparations thereof	472	556	762
Vegetables and fruit	442	931	1,128
Coffee, tea, cocoa, spices and manufactures thereof	157	241	313
Miscellaneous edible products and preparations	62	88	177
Others	285	311	503
Sub-total	**1,418**	**2,128**	**2,883**
Beverages and tobacco			
Beverages	92	111	129
Tobacco and tobacco manufactures	200	356	395
Sub-total	**291**	**466**	**524**
Crude materials, inedible, except fuels			
Textile fibres (other than wool tops) and their wastes (not manufactured into yarn or fabrics)	463	694	434
Metalliferous ores and metal scrap	343	606	306
Crude animal and vegetable materials, n e s	1,165	1,249	1,565
Others	402	699	647
Sub-total	**2,373**	**3,249**	**3,002**
Mineral fuels, lubricants and related materials			
Petroleum, petroleum products and related materials	325	434	489
Others	7	10	17
Sub-total	**332**	**444**	**506**
Animal and vegetable oils, fats and waxes	**46**	**59**	**107**
Chemicals and related products, n e s			
Dyeing, tanning and colouring materials	462	658	766
Medicinal and pharmaceutical products	594	758	794
Artificial resins and plastic materials, and cellulose esters and ethers	427	544	542
Others	1,333	1,621	1,807
Sub-total	**2,817**	**3,581**	**3,909**

Manufactured goods classified chiefly by material			
Textile yarn, fabrics, made-up articles, n e s and related products	4,310	6,931	6,431
Non-metallic mineral manufactures, n e s	2,388	2,708	2,565
Non-ferrous metals	596	514	732
Manufactures of metal, n e s	590	960	1,132
Others	878	1,069	1,140
Sub-total	**8,762**	**12,233**	**12,000**
Machinery and transport equipment			
Telecommunications and sound recording and reproducing apparatus and equipment	1,283	2,123	1,697
Electrical machinery, apparatus and appliances, n e s, and electrical parts thereof	1,963	3,069	3,420
Road vehicles (including air-cushion vehicles)	1,218	2,340	2,302
Others	2,298	2,882	3,486
Sub-total	**6,762**	**10,415**	**10,905**
Miscellaneous manufactured articles			
Articles of apparel and clothing accessories	1,554	2,197	3,021
Footwear	215	350	480
Photographic apparatus, equipment and supplies and optical goods, n e s; watches and clocks	2,810	3,393	3,218
Miscellaneous manufactured articles, n e s	1,392	1,954	2,412
Others	593	884	1,254
Sub-total	**6,565**	**8,788**	**10,385**
Commodities and transactions not classified according to kind	706	378	132
Total merchandise	**30,072**	**41,739**	**44,353**
Gold and specie	3,008	218	2,285
Grand total	**33,080**	**41,957**	**46,637**

Note: n e s = not elsewhere specified.

Source: *Hong Kong Annual Report 1983.* (Hong Kong: Government Printer, 1983)

Table 2.8: Re-exports by Countries

Re-exports

Destination	1977 $	1977 %	1978 $	1978 %	1979 $	1979 %
Japan	1,339	13.6	2,282	17.3	2,477	12.4
United States	883	9.0	1,232	9.3	1,995	10.0
Singapore	1,063	10.8	1,390	10.5	1,804	9.0
Taiwan	872	8.9	1,221	9.3	1,730	8.6
Indonesia	1,059	10.8	1,302	9.9	1,684	8.4
China	175	1.8	214	1.6	1,315	6.6
Republic of Korea (South Korea)	456	4.6	600	4.5	818	4.1
Philippines	331	3.4	507	3.8	777	3.9
Macau	318	3.2	358	2.7	605	3.0
Thailand	360	3.7	368	2.8	542	2.7
Others	2,975	30.3	3,724	28.2	6,276	31.3
Merchandise total	9,829	100.0	13,197	100.0	20,022	100.0

Destination	1980 $	%	1981 $	%	1982 $	%
China	4,642	15.4	8,044	19.3	7,992	18.0
United States	3,085	10.3	4,785	11.5	5,615	12.7
Indonesia	2,761	9.2	4,272	10.2	4,615	10.4
Singapore	2,510	8.3	3,243	7.8	3,648	8.2
Taiwan	2,229	7.4	2,420	5.8	2,662	6.0
Japan	2,201	7.3	2,792	6.7	2,566	5.8
Republic of Korea (South Korea)	899	3.0	1,401	3.4	1,699	3.8
Macau	923	3.1	1,407	3.4	1,588	3.6
Philippines	904	3.0	1,294	3.1	1,485	3.3
Saudi Arabia	345	1.1	582	1.4	941	2.1
Others	9,573	31.8	11,500	27.5	11,543	26.0
Merchandise total	30,072	100.0	41,739	100.0	44,353	100.0

Source: *Hong Kong Trade Statistics*, various years, (Hong Kong: Government Printer, 1977-83)

Table 3.1: Distribution of Usable Responses of the Questionnaire by Industry

Industry	Number of Usable Responses	Percentage of Total
Clothing	32	70%
Electronics	14	30
Total	46	100%

Table 3.2: Distribution of Firms Interviewed by Industry

Industry	Number of Firms Interviewed	Percentage of Total
Clothing	6	60%
Electronics	4	40
Total	10	100%

Figure 4.1: Some Alternative Export Channels of Distribution

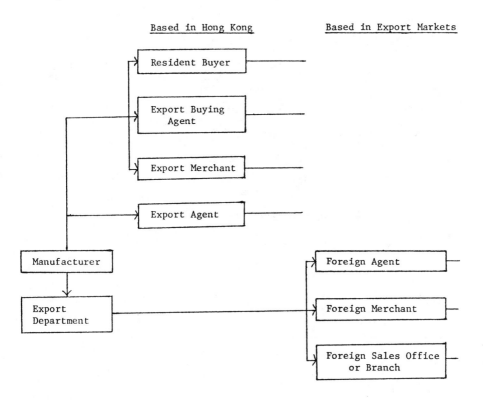

Table 4.1: Perceived Performance of the Industries and Firms

A. Perceived Performance of the Industries

| | Clothing | | Electronics | |
	No.	%	No.	%
Very successful	2	6.3	6	42.9
Quite successful	22	68.8	8	57.1
Average	8	25.0	0	0.0
Total	32	100.0	14	100.0

B. Perceived Performance of the Firms

| | Clothing | | Electronics | |
	No.	%	No.	%
Above Average	20	62.5	9	64.3
Average	12	37.5	5	35.7
Total	32	100.0	14	100.0

Table 4.2: Export Experience and Future Expectations

A. Changes in Company Goals Regarding Export Program

	Clothing		Electronics	
	No.	%	No.	%
Moved towards expansion	18	56.2	10	71.4
Remained the same	14	43.8	4	28.6
Total	32	100.0	14	100.0

B. Importance of Various Marketing Variables for Export Expansion

	Levels of Importance					
	Clothing			Electronics		
	Highly Impt.	Impt.	Slightly Impt.	Highly Impt.	Impt.	Slightly Impt.
	No. %	No. %	No. %	No. %	No. %	No. %
Product	20 62.5	12 37.5	0 0.0	13 92.9	1 7.1	0 0.0
Distribution	18 56.3	14 43.7	0 0.0	10 71.4	4 28.6	0 0.0
Price	13 40.6	19 59.4	0 0.0	4 28.6	10 71.4	0 0.0
Promotion	0 0.0	20 62.5	12 37.5	0 0.0	12 85.7	2 14.3

C. Perceived Hindrance of International Environmental Factors

	Clothing		Electronics	
	Points*	Rank	Points*	Rank
Cultural Difference	2	5	5	5
Quotas & Tariffs	40	1	7	3
Foreign Competition	23	3	30	2
Market Demand	30	2	50	1
Transportation	5	4	8	4
	100		100	

*More·points indicate greater hindrance

Table 4.2 (continued)

D. The Proportion of Export Channel Functions Performed as a Result
   of Increase in Overseas Competition and Trade Restrictions

	Clothing		Electronics	
	No.	%	No.	%
Increased substantially	8	25.0	7	50.0
Increased moderately	11	34.4	3	21.4
Remained unchanged	13	40.6	4	28.6
Total	32	100.0	14	100.0

Table 4.3: Perceived Performance, Average Export Sales, Emphasis on Distribution and Export Program Goals

A. Perceived Performance and Export Program Goals

	Perceived Performance			
	Above Average		Average	
Goals Regarding Export Program	No.	%	No.	%
Moved toward expansion	23	79.3	5	29.4
Remained the same	6	20.7	12	70.6
Total	29	100.0	17	100.0

Chi-square = 9.206, with one degree of freedom*

B. Average Export Sales and Export Program Goals

	Average Export Sales (Annual)			
	HK$ 50 Million & Over		Below HK$ 50 Million	
Goals Regarding Export Program	No.	%	No.	%
Moved toward expansion	16	80.0	12	46.2
Remained the same	4	20.0	14	53.8
Total	20	100.0	26	100.0

Chi-square = 4.108, with one degree of freedom**

C. Export Program Goals and Emphasis on Distribution

	Export Program Goals			
	Moved toward Expansion		Remained the Same	
Emphasis on Distribution	No.	%	No.	%
Highly Important	22	78.6	6	33.3
Important	6	21.4	12	66.7
Total	28	100.0	18	100.0

Chi-square = 7.610, with one degree of freedom*

*Significant at the 1% level   **Significant at the 5% level

Table 4.4: Foreign Competition, Trade Restrictions, and Export Channel Functions

A. Foreign Competition and Export Channel Functions

Proportion of Export Channel Functions	Concern About Foreign Competition			
	More Concerned		Less Concerned	
	No.	%	No.	%
Increased	23	82.1	6	33.3
Unchanged	5	17.9	12	66.7
Total	28	100.0	18	100.0

Chi-square = 9.206, with one degree of freedom*

B. Trade Restrictions and Export Channel Functions

Proportion of Export Channel Functions	Concern About Trade Restrictions			
	More Concerned		Less Concerned	
	No.	%	No.	%
Increased	16	80.0	13	50.0
Unchanged	4	20.0	13	50.0
Total	20	100.0	26	100.0

Chi-square = 3.174, with one degree of freedom**

*Significant at the 1% level
**Significant at the 10% level

Table 4.5: Allocation of Executives' Time for Export Matters

Executives' Time for Export Matters	During Initial Years of Export Operations				During Current Years of Export Operations			
	Clothing		Electronics		Clothing		Electronics	
	No.	%	No.	%	No.	%	No.	%
Full-time	20	37.5	10	71.4	28	87.5	14	100.0
Part-time	12	62.5	4	28.6	4	12.5	0	0.0
Total	32	100.0	14	100.0	32	100.0	14	100.0

Table 4.6: Structure of Export Channels During the Initial and the Current Years of Export Operations

Portion of Export Channel Functions Handled by	Clothing				Electronics			
	YES		NO		YES		NO	
	No.	%	No.	%	No.	%	No.	%
	During Initial Years of Export Operations							
Hong Kong Based Resident Buyer	20	62.5	12	37.5	10	71.4	4	28.6
Hong Kong Based Buying Agent	10	31.3	22	68.7	2	14.3	12	85.7
Hong Kong Based Merchant	19	59.4	13	40.6	4	28.6	10	71.4
Hong Kong Based Agent	14	43.8	18	56.2	4	28.6	10	71.4
Firm's Export Department	22	68.8	10	31.2	10	71.4	4	28.6
Foreign Based Agent	6	18.8	26	81.2	2	14.3	12	85.7
Foreign Based Merchant	4	12.5	28	87.5	2	14.3	12	85.7
Firm's Foreign Sales Office	0	0.0	32	100.0	2	14.3	12	85.7
	During Current Years of Export Operations							
Hong Kong Based Resident Buyer	26	81.3	6	18.7	10	71.4	4	28.6
Hong Kong Based Buying Agent	12	37.5	20	62.5	2	14.3	12	85.7
Hong Kong Based Merchant	18	56.3	14	43.7	6	42.9	8	57.1
Hong Kong Based Agent	16	50.0	16	50.0	4	28.6	10	71.4
Firm's Export Department	28	87.5	4	12.5	14	100.0	0	0.0
Foreign Based Agent	10	31.3	22	68.7	4	28.6	10	71.4
Foreign Based Merchant	12	37.5	20	62.5	4	28.6	10	71.4
Firm's Foreign Sales Office	10	31.3	22	68.7	8	57.1	6	42.9

Table 4.7: Sales Offices or Branches in Foreign Markets

A. The Establishment of Sales Offices or Branches in Foreign Markets

	Clothing		Electronics	
	No.	%	No.	%
Had Established Offices Abroad	10	31.3	8	57.1
Had not set up Offices Abroad	22	68.7	6	42.9
Total	32	100.0	14	100.0

B. For the 28 Firms that did not set up any Offices Abroad, Plan in the Coming 5 Years

	Clothing		Electronics	
	No.	%	No.	%
Likely to set up Offices Abroad	6	27.3	3	50.0
Undecided	9	40.9	1	16.7
Unlikely to set up Offices Abroad	7	31.8	2	33.3
Total	22	100.0	6	100.0

Table 4.8: Number of Alternative Channels Considered

Number of Alternative Channels Considered	During Initial Years of Export Operations				During Current Years of Export Operations			
	Clothing		Electronics		Clothing		Electronics	
	No.	%	No.	%	No.	%	No.	%
Two	4	12.5	2	14.3	2	6.2	0	0.0
Three	8	25.0	0	0.0	2	6.2	0	0.0
Four	14	43.8	2	14.3	10	31.3	2	14.2
Five	2	6.3	8	57.1	6	18.8	6	42.9
Over Five	4	12.4	2	14.3	12	37.5	6	42.9
Total	32	100.0	14	100.0	32	100.0	14	100.0

Table 4.9: Criteria for Selecting Export Distribution Channels

Selective Criteria	Clothing				Electronics			
	YES		NO		YES		NO	
	No.	%	No.	%	No.	%	No.	%
During Initial Years of Export Operations								
Market Potential	20	62.5	12	37.5	12	85.7	2	14.3
Market Area Served	22	68.8	10	31.2	2	14.3	12	85.7
Growth Plan	0	0.0	32	100.0	0	0.0	14	100.0
Experience	16	50.0	16	50.0	4	28.6	10	71.4
Financial Strength	8	25.0	24	75.0	6	42.9	8	57.1
During Current Years of Export Operations								
Market Potential	20	62.5	12	37.5	12	85.7	2	14.3
Market Area Served	26	81.2	6	18.8	8	57.1	6	42.9
Growth Plan	4	12.5	28	87.5	0	0.0	14	100.0
Experience	22	68.8	10	31.2	6	42.9	8	57.1
Financial Strength	18	56.3	14	43.7	8	57.1	6	42.9

Table 4.10: Executives' Involvement in Channel Evaluation

Executives' Involvement	Clothing				Electronics			
	YES		NO		YES		NO	
	No.	%	No.	%	No.	%	No.	%
Top Management	30	93.8	2	6.2	12	85.7	2	14.3
Accounting	0	0.0	32	100.0	2	14.3	12	85.7
Marketing	6	18.8	26	81.2	4	28.6	10	71.4
Production	10	31.3	22	68.7	2	14.3	12	85.7
Finance	2	6.2	30	93.8	0	0.0	14	100.0
Sales	14	43.8	18	56.2	4	28.6	10	71.4

Table 4.11: Frequency and Duration of Channel Evaluation

A. Frequency of Channel Evaluation

Frequency of Evaluation	Clothing		Electronics	
	No.	%	No.	%
More Frequent	14	43.7	11	78.6
Less Frequent	18	56.3	3	21.4
Total	32	100.0	14	100.0

B. Amount of Time Spent on Evaluating Channels

Time Spent on Evaluation	Clothing		Electronics	
	No.	%	No.	%
Substantial Amount	11	34.4	10	71.4
Minimal Amount	21	65.6	4	28.6
Total	32	100.0	14	100.0

Table 4.12: Criteria for Evaluating Performance of Export Channels

Evaluative Criteria	Clothing				Electronics			
	YES		NO		YES		NO	
	No.	%	No.	%	No.	%	No.	%
Market Share	18	56.2	14	43.8	10	71.4	4	28.6
Gross Margin	22	68.8	10	31.2	4	28.6	10	71.4
Investment	8	25.0	24	75.0	4	28.6	10	71.4
Cost	20	62.5	12	37.5	10	71.4	4	28.6
Sales	22	68.8	10	31.2	6	42.9	8	57.1

Table 4.13: Perceived Performance of Channel Intermediaries

Perceived Attributes	Clothing						Electronics					
	Highly Satisf.		Satisf.		Dis-Satisf.		Satisf.		Satisf.		Dis-Satisf.	
	No.	%	No.	%	No.	%	No.	%	No.	%	No.	%
Cooperativeness	2	6.3	26	81.2	4	12.5	2	14.3	8	57.1	4	28.6
Dependability	2	6.3	22	68.7	8	25.0	0	0.0	8	57.1	6	42.9
Intelligence	0	0.0	28	87.5	4	12.5	2	14.3	12	85.7	0	0.0
Competence	4	12.5	24	75.0	4	12.5	0	0.0	12	85.7	2	14.3

Table 4.14: Events Leading to Channel Modification

Events Leading to Channel Modification	Clothing				Electronics			
	YES		NO		YES		NO	
	No.	%	No.	%	No.	%	No.	%
Changes in Demand	18	56.2	14	43.8	8	57.1	6	42.9
Product Changes	8	25.0	24	75.0	4	28.6	10	71.4
Competition	14	43.8	18	56.2	6	42.9	8	57.1
New Markets	16	50.0	16	50.0	8	57.1	6	42.9
Changes in Sales	10	31.3	22	68.8	2	14.3	12	85.7
Changes in Profitability	8	25.0	24	75.0	2	14.3	12	85.7
Customer Needs	18	56.2	14	43.8	6	42.9	8	57.1
Loss of Market Share	4	12.5	28	87.5	2	14.3	12	85.7
Changes in Costs	10	31.3	22	68.8	4	28.6	10	71.4

Table 4.15: Channel Involvement and Firm Characteristics

	Degree of Channel Involvement			
	High Involvement		Low Involvement	
	No.	%	No.	%
A. Ownership Status				
Public-owned	2	7.1	2	11.1
Private-owned	26	92.9	16	88.9
Total	28	100.0	18	100.0

Chi-square = 0.005, with one degree of freedom

B. Export Experience				
Under 10 Years	12	42.9	10	55.6
10 Years or Above	16	57.1	8	44.4
Total	28	100.0	18	100.0

Chi-square = 0.290, with one degree of freedom

C. Export Sales Growth				
Under 10 Percent	14	50.0	5	27.8
10 Percent or Above	14	50.0	13	72.2
Total	28	100.0	18	100.0

Chi-square = 1.409, with one degree of freedom

D. Average Annual Export Sales				
Below HK$ 50 Million	12	42.9	14	77.8
HK$ 50 Million or Above	16	57.1	4	22.2
Total	28	100.0	18	100.0

Chi-square = 4.108, with one degree of freedom*

Table 4.15 (continued)

	High Involvement		Low Involvement	
	No.	%	No.	%
E. Size of Operations				
Below 200 Workers	6	21.4	10	55.6
200 Workers or Above	22	78.6	8	44.4
Total	28	100.0	18	100.0

Chi-square = 4.221, with one degree of freedom*

*Significant at the 5% level

Table 4.16: Firm Characteristics and Channel Evaluation

A. Export Sales Growth and Frequency of Evaluation

	Export Sales Growth			
Frequency	10 Percent and Over		Below 10 Percent	
of Evaluation	No.	%	No.	%
More Frequent	16	59.3	9	47.5
Less Frequent	11	40.7	10	52.6
Total	27	100.0	19	100.0

Chi-square = 0.247, with one degree of freedom

B. Average Annual Export Sales and Frequency of Evaluation

	Average Annual Export Sales			
Frequency	HK$ 50 Million & Over		Below HK$ 50 Million	
of Evaluation	No.	%	No.	%
More Frequent	16	80.0	9	34.6
Less Frequent	4	20.0	17	65.4
Total	20	100.0	26	100.0

Chi-square = 7.645, with one degree of freedom*

C. Size of Operations and Frequency of Evaluation

	Size of Operations			
Frequency	200 Workers & Over		Below 200 Workers	
	No.	%	No.	%
More Frequent	20	66.7	5	31.2
Less Frequent	10	33.3	11	68.8
Total	30	100.0	16	100.0

Chi-square = 3.945, with one degree of freedom**

*Significant at the 1% level
**Significant at the 5% level

Table 4.17: Channel Evaluation and Channel Involvement

| Degree of Channel Involvement | Frequency of Evaluation | | | |
| | More Frequent | | Less Frequent | |
	No.	%	No.	%
High Involvement	21	84.0	7	33.3
Low Involvement	4	16.0	14	66.7
Total	25	100.0	21	100.0

Chi-square = 10.256, with one degree of freedom*

*Significant at the 1% level

4

Findings and Discussion

This chapter presents an analysis of the survey data and an outline of the study's findings. The results from the questionnaire survey and the personal interviews are examined at various phases of the analysis.

Three phases of analysis can be distinguished. The first phase describes historical perspectives for the two manufacturing industries under investigation, clothing and electronics. Background information regarding history of the two industries is discussed. Special emphasis is placed on export sales and market structure, and the current status in terms of factors which contribute to growth and development is discussed.

The second phase involves a cross-sectional analysis of how the two industries view various issues in export distribution channels. Responses are arranged by industry so that the extent and significance of differences among the two industries can be detected.

The final phase of the analysis explores the relationships between channel involvement, channel evaluation, and specific characteristics of the firm, namely ownership, export experience, export sales growth, average annual export sales, and size of operation.

Chi-square analysis is the statistical tool used for testing the significance of relationships in the analysis. The use of chi-square can help to determine whether a systematic relationship exists between two variables. Small values of chi-square indicate the absence of a relationship, often referred to as statistical independence. On the other hand, a large chi-square suggests the presence of systematic relationship between the variables.[1]

Historical Perspectives of Hong Kong's Clothing and Electronics Industries

The Clothing Industry

Historical review. The first clothing factory was established in the early 1930s, producing a limited quantity of low quality items with manual machines. During the 1950s, with the increase in orders flowing in from the United States and Western Europe, production skills, machines and equipment were improved and modernized. Most manufacturers moved toward more automation and adopted the assembly line concept. As a result, the productivity of Hong Kong's clothing industry increased drastically, and the improved quality of exports was welcomed by foreign buyers. In recent years, the clothing industry has become the leading industry in Hong Kong in terms of export value, number of establishments and employment of workers.

During the 1950s, the exports of the clothing industry has been primarily cotton clothing. Since the early 1960s, the growing protectionism sentiments in the United States and Western Europe had resulted in restrictions on international trade in cotton textiles. The immediate impact of the first restriction was the increased use of manmade fibers in clothing exports. However, moving into the 1970s, the Multi-Fiber Arrangement put restriction on exports of clothing made by manmade fibers as well.[2]

During recent years, most Hong Kong clothing manufacturers have been working toward the production of high quality fashion. The clothing industry shed its shoddy image and earned recognition from foreign retailers for the quality of Hong Kong clothing. The successful staging of fashion promotion overseas has earned high recognition for Hong Kong clothing, attracting many internationally known fashion brandnames who buy from, or produce, in Hong Kong. The exports of the clothing industry include a wide variety of products: shirts, slacks, jackets and other outer garments, pajamas, raincoats and high fashion dresses. Exports of clothing to the United States, West Germany and the United Kingdom accounted for over 60 percent of total value of clothing exports over the fifteen years from 1968 to 1982. This reflects the underlying strong demand from and Hong Kong's dependence upon these three major markets.

Beginning in 1975, there has been a gradual trend among Hong Kong clothing manufacturers to adopt new and advanced machines and equipment. According to one of the executives interviewed, new machines can be classified as fully automatic or semi-automatic. Fully automatic machines can produce finished goods with a minimal amount of labor input. Semi-automatic machines facilitate and expedite several manufacturing processes in clothing production such as cutting and trimming. Currently, approximately ten large clothing manufacturing firms utilize fully automatic equipment, whereas about one-third of the average sized firms use semi-automatic machines. The use of the sophisticated and advanced machines and equipment improves efficiency and effectiveness of these firms, leading to higher productivity and better quality which enable the firms to compete with clothing firms from other countries for export markets more effectively.

Export sales and markets. During 1982, domestic exports of clothing were valued at HK$ 28,824 million, compared with HK$ 28,288 million in 1981.[3] The United States absorbed 40 percent of the total with a value of HK$ 11,594 million.[4] The European Economic Community imported HK$ 9,292 million of Hong Kong clothing, West Germany imported HK$ 4,333 million and the United Kingdom absorbed HK$ 3,381 million. Japan was the fourth largest importer of Hong Kong clothing, with a value of HK$ 1,268 million, followed by Canada with HK$ 921 million.

Looking at exports of clothing by category, textile clothing such as cotton, silk, and manmade fibers for men and women accounted for the largest share at HK$ 26,243 million or 91 percent of total clothing exports. However, in recent years, the fur clothing industry has seen rapid growth and 1982's exports were valued at HK$ 1,086 million. Leather clothing exports were worth HK$ 222 million, and clothing accessories amounted to HK$ 1,223 million in 1982.

Although the export performance of the clothing industry has been increasing over the years, the profit earnings for different manufacturers vary a great deal. According to most of the executives interviewed, the rate of increase in material and labor costs has surpassed the rate of increase in prices of clothing exports. For the larger firms which produce high quality, high priced items, net profit could be higher with the increase in overseas orders. However, the smaller firms must purchase a large quantity of quotas in order to accept large orders, which further increases the cost of exports, leading to a lower profit rate. A discussion of current modifications in Hong Kong's quota allocation system is in Appendix IX.

Current status. Moving into the 1980s, the clothing industry continues to grow steadily. Men's clothing, which had been insignificant in the past, continues to move toward becoming the fastest growing component of clothing exports.

Looking at the European Economic Community (E.E.C.), strong appreciation of the British pound and German mark against the Hong Kong dollar has increased the attractiveness of Hong Kong clothing. In addition, there has been an increasing trend of Hong Kong clothing being re-exported from the United Kingdom and West Germany to Africa, the Middle East and East Germany. Together with the Hong Kong clothing manufacturers' ability to produce high quality goods and provide punctual delivery, these conditions should bring about a higher growth for clothing exports to the E.E.C. Under such circumstances, firms that have limited quota allocation for E.E.C. markets pay high prices in acquiring quotas from other manufacturers. According to one of the executives interviewed, many firms have to buy a sufficient amount of quotas before accepting orders, which requires extensive capital investments, as foreign buyers will place an order only if the manufacturers have the quotas to fill it.

Exports to the United States will show some improvement pending the recovery of U.S. economy. The transfer prices of export quotas for the United States have fluctuated significantly. Buyers in the United States have been ordering three months in advance instead of six-month period, resulting in lower levels of inventory that necessitate frequent short notice orders to replenish empty stocks. Hong Kong is in an advantageous position over its competitors in South Korea and Taiwan, who are unable to accept such short notice orders. However, the low wage rates in South Korea, Taiwan and Philippines allow firms in these countries to attract a large portion of orders for low priced clothing items away from Hong Kong.

The higher wage rate in Hong Kong, as well as the increasing costs of imported materials, represent the key problems facing Hong Kong's clothing industry. In addition, the high turnover rate of workers also creates operating problems. One executive mentioned that firms are hesitant to accept orders up to their full production levels, for fear of turnover and shortages of workers that are likely to cause delay in shipment via sea routes. The additional costs of air freight would definitely cut into the profit margin or even move the firm into the loss column.

Looking forward into the 1980s, the clothing industry should continue to grow. More and more firms are switching away from low priced items to high quality, high priced fashions, which are gaining acceptance from foreign buyers. The influx of refugees from China and Vietnam can help to solve the labor shortages given that the necessary training is provided to them. In addition, with the continuing decline in inventory stocks among export markets, orders coming from the United States and E.E.C. are increasing significantly.

The Electronics Industry

Historical review. The electronics industry in Hong Kong began in the late 1950s with only a few small establishments assembling simple transistor radios. During the past ten years, rapid growth and development have moved the electronics industry into the second position among Hong Kong industries.

The development of Hong Kong's electronics industry can be roughly divided into three stages: (1) from the late 1950s through 1965, the industry began its initial stage with approximately 20 to 30 factories engaging solely in the assembling of transistor radios; (2) the second half of the 1960s saw the beginning of production of transistor radios and electronic calculators, in addition to expansion of assembling capacity of the industry; and (3) with the continuing growth and development, heavy investments, made beginning in 1970, create a highly competitive industry which incorporates high technology to produce a wide variety of products.

According to statistics from the Hong Kong Census and Statistics Department, there were three factories in 1960 employing 170 workers and exporting a total of HK$ 13 million worth of transistor radios. The value of exports increased to HK$ 558 million in 1968, with 109 factories employing 30,600 workers.[5] This represented a growth rate of 43 times in export value, approximately 36 times in the number of factories and 180 times in the number of workers. By 1978, the number of factories had increased to 842, employing a total of 74,530 workers and exporting HK$ 4,741 million worth of electronic products. By this time, electronic exports had already expanded to include components and parts for computers, transistors, diodes, and integrated circuits. Domestic exports of electronics increased to HK$ 15,982 million in 1982, compared to HK$ 15,774 million in 1981. The industry employed 85,946 workers in 1,305 factories in 1982.[6]

Since the 1970s, the scale of operations in the electronics industry has been increasing, with a wide variety of high quality products being manufactured. Besides the outstanding performance of Hong Kong's exports of electronic watches, the range of products includes radios, computer memory systems, calculators, transistors, integrated circuits, semi-conductors, prepackaged electronic modules, television sets, smoke detectors, and burglar alarm systems. In addition, the output of the electronics industry has been facilitating the expansion of several other Hong Kong industries. For example, the rapid development of electronic toys shows the result of the development of Hong Kong's electronics industry.

Export sales and markets. During 1982, most electronic products experienced slight increases in export sales. Total exports of electronics were HK$ 15,986 million, this was equivalent to 19 percent of Hong Kong's domestic exports.[7] Electronics exports to the United States were valued at HK$ 7,409 million or 46 percent of the total. West Germany ranked second with HK$ 1,155 million worth of Hong Kong electronics, followed by the United Kingdom with HK$ 979 million. China, at fourth place, imported HK$ 755 million, and Canada accounted for HK$ 582 million.

Consumer electronics accounted for 74 percent of Hong Kong's electronic exports, major products were transistor radios, electronic calculators, and cassette tape recorders. Industrial electronics, namely industrial controls, electronic inspection systems, electronic test and measuring equipment, data processing systems, and communication systems, made up the remaining 26 percent of Hong Kong's electronics exports.

The export statistics show that there is a heavy concentration of export markets for Hong Kong's electronic outputs. One of the executives interviewed mentioned that although the number of export markets had increased from around 80 in 1966 to over 120 in 1982, the three major markets—the United States, West Germany and United Kingdom—together accounted for about 60 percent of all electronic exports from Hong Kong. In the event that economic recession or increasing protectionism affect any of these markets, there will be serious adverse effects on the electronics industry of Hong Kong.

Current status. Moving into the 1980s, the electronics industry continues to maintain a steady growth rate. Looking at export statistics for the first four months of 1983, exports of electronic products showed expansion over the same period in 1982.

Over the years, the success of the electronics industry has been attributed to the advancement in the use of technology and the trend of producing and developing high quality products. According to one of the executives interviewed, the larger and more successful firms are moving toward adding capacity to produce more computer parts and components, which already account for 20 percent of total electronic exports. The forecast is that the percentage can increase to as high as 50 percent by 1985.

There are several underlying problems facing the electronics industry of Hong Kong. The most obvious is the shortage of skilled labor and the resulting high turnover rate. According to the survey results of the Hong Kong Census and Statistic Department, the number of job vacancies in the electronics industry were approximately 5,000 in 1980, which included mainly technicians, craftsmen and semi-skilled operative workers.[8] The shortages in skilled and semi-skilled workers triggered a "wage war" among electronics manufacturers and pushed the average rate to a 30 percent increase. The higher wages cut into the manufacturers' profit margins and force increases in export prices of electronics. In addition, the impact of the Organization for Petroleum Exporting Countries' oil price increase in 1979 brought about the drastic price increases of some important inputs, such as plastic raw materials, as well as the recession in the economies of major export markets.

Continuing into the 1980s, the outputs and export sales of the electronics industry are expected to show steady improvements. However, the underlying problems will also intensify, resulting in less spectacular growth.

Export Channel Strategy of Clothing and Electronics Firms

The data for the remaining sections of the analysis were collected by questionnaire survey and personal interviews. A total of 200 clothing and electronics firms were selected for the questionnaire survey, and the 46 usable responses included 32 clothing firms and 14 electronics firms. Fifteen of the questionnaire survey respondents were approached before ten firms decided to participate in the interview process. Six of the firms interviewed were from the clothing industry, and the remaining firms were manufacturers of electronics.

Perceived Performance of the Industries and Firms

Success of the Hong Kong manufacturing firms depends on their capability to adapt to changes in export markets and international environmental forces, which include the industry of which the firm is a part. Management decision making is influenced by development in the industry. Therefore, it is important to consider how the firms view the performance of their industries in recent years and how the firms perceive their own performance relative to "average" firms in their respective industries.

Looking at table 4.1, section A shows that 43 percent of electronics firms rated the performance of their industry as very successful, compared to only 6 percent for the clothing industry.[9] The remaining 57 percent of electronics firms and 69 percent of the clothing firms viewed their respective industries as quite successful. Twenty-five percent of the clothing firms rated the performance of the clothing industry as only "average." One of the executives interviewed suggested that the insufficient allocation of export quotas and the limit imposed on growth of quotas probably accounted for the "average" responses from some clothing manufacturing firms.

On the other hand, section B lists the perceived performance of the firms relative to "average" firms in their respective industries. About 63 percent of the clothing firms and 64 percent of the electronic firms perceived the performance of their firms as above average. The remaining 38 and 36 percent of clothing and electronics firms respectively viewed their performance as comparable to "average" firms in their industries. One executive interviewed suggested that the ability to generate a high export volume may be a significant factor in explaining the high ratings of the above-average group.

Export Experience and Future Expectations

In order to gain insight into the firms' export experience and their future expectations, several questions were asked in the questionnaire which required each firm to:

1. evaluate changes that have taken place in the firm's goals regarding its export program,
2. rate the importance of various marketing variables, supposing that the firm decided to expand its export program,
3. rank several international environmental factors which hinder the firm's export distribution, and
4. assess the proportion of export channel functions performed by the firm with the increase in overseas competition and trade restrictions in importing countries.

The responses are tabulated in table 4.2. Section A indicates 56 percent of the clothing firms reported changes toward expansion in company goals regarding export program over the past four years. The percentage of electronics firms that changed their company goals toward expanding export programs was slightly higher at 61 percent. The remaining 44 and 39 percent of clothing and electronics firms respectively reported no change in this area of their company goals.

Section B of table 4.2 shows the result of comparison regarding the importance of various marketing variables. Product (e.g., product improvement) was rated as highly important by 93 percent of the electronics firms, compared to 63 percent for clothing firms. The remaining 7 percent of firms in electronics and 37 percent of firms in clothing viewed product as important.

Distribution (e.g., channel management) was rated highly important of 56 and 71 percent of the firms in clothing and electronics respectively. The remaining firms in the clothing and the electronics industries viewed distribution as important.

Price (e.g., price discount) received a rating of highly important from 41 percent of the clothing firms and 29 percent of the electronics firms. Promotion (e.g., additional allocation) received no highly important rating, with 63 percent of the clothing firms and 86 percent of the electronics firms rating it as important.

When considering the expansion of the export program, product is rated as the most important marketing variable in terms of the percentage of highly important ratings received. Distribution is second, followed by price, and then promotion. The offering of products by the firms in overseas markets obviously is the most important aspect of exporting. However, the second highest rating for distribution suggests that the Hong Kong manufacturing firms are placing increasing emphasis on channels of distribution as a strategy for expanding export program. The growing acceptance of the quality of higher priced Hong Kong clothing and electronics reduces the importance of pricing strategy. The number of markets and the communication gaps between the markets and the manufacturers make export promotion an extremely difficult function, and most Hong Kong manufacturers tend to place less emphasis on promotion.

As far as the clothing industry is concerned, quotas and tariffs represented the greatest hindrance among four other international environmental factors. The ranking continued with market demand, foreign competition, transportation costs and cultural differences, which followed in that order as reported in table 4.2 (section C). With the clothing exports facing restrictions from major export markets under the Multi-Fiber Arrangement, the growth of the clothing industry is hampered.

Firms in the electronics industry placed market demand ahead of foreign competition in terms of hindrance in export distribution, followed by quotas and tariffs, transportation costs, and then cultural differences. Most orders in electronics involve detailed specifications and are often made to order. Decline in market demand will force the firms to operate below capacity and fall behind in the technological race. Given the advancement of technology in electronics, outputs can become obsolete much faster when compared to outputs from the clothing industry. Quotas and tariffs received a much lower ranking because only a small fraction of Hong Kong's electronic exports is subjected to restrictions in importing countries.

As shown in section D of table 4.2, 59 percent of the clothing firms and 71 percent of the electronics firms reported moderate or substantial increases in the proportion of export channel functions performed as a result of increase in overseas competition and trade restrictions. The remaining 41 and 29 percent of clothing and electronics firms respectively indicated no change in the proportion of export channel functions they performed. By providing financial incentives or other services, the Hong Kong manufacturing firms are absorbing export channel functions from existing channel agencies or institutions, which results in these firms being more attractive to export channel intermediaries. The recent development of the electronics industry in the 1970s suggests that electronics manufacturers have been expanding their export programs more aggressively than clothing manufacturers. The long history of the clothing industry can partially explain the conservative nature of most clothing manufacturing firms in Hong Kong.

Factors Influencing Formulation of Export Channel Strategy

The importance of an effective channel strategy for export distribution has been discussed in chapter 1. However, the success of a firm's effort to select an effective channel strategy depends on its management's ability to identify and adapt to forces influencing the formulation of export channel strategy. By cross tabulating responses according to export experience and future expectations of the firms, insights into the factors which influence or are associated with how the Hong Kong manufacturing firms formulate export channel strategy may be gained.

It is frequently suggested that the larger and more successful firms formulate channel strategy for export distribution based upon company goals and major forces in the international environment. The rationale behind this is that their larger size and greater success reflects effective management, which necessitates a correspondingly high degree of sophistication on the part of management to formulate strategy that can achieve the desired objectives. The goals of firms engaging in exporting typically change as the volume of exports increases. This implies that the selection of export channel strategy is a function of company goals.

Because the export of products to overseas markets moves the firms into the arena of international operations, the marketing environment will be complicated by cultural and economic forces, foreign competition, and other political and institutional forces. Therefore, the formulation of channel strategy for export distribution is affected by forces in the international environment.

Underlying the foregoing discussion are the first two hypotheses of the study, which are re-stated as follows:

Hypothesis 1:   As the volume of exports increases, goals of the larger and more successful Hong Kong manufacturing firms will become more committed to expanding their export programs leading to greater emphasis on distribution channel strategy.

Hypothesis 2:   The larger and more successful Hong Kong manufacturing firms will respond to increases in overseas competition and trade restrictions in importing countries by performing an increased proportion of channel functions, such as financing inventory, financing and developing promotional programs, and other service or financial functions for agencies or institutions in the existing export channel structures.

To test these hypotheses, responses from the questionnaire associated with perceived performance of the firm, average annual export sales, and the firm's emphasis on distribution were related to changes in the firm's goals regarding export program. In addition, responses to questions associated with emphasis on foreign competition and trade restrictions were related to differences in the proportion of export channel functions performed by the firm. The chi-square test was used to examine the significance of relationships.

Table 4.3 provides the cross tabulated data that relate the perceived performance of the firms, the average annual export sales, and the firms' emphasis on distribution to the firms' goals regarding export program.[10] Section A shows a significant association (at 1% level) between the perceived performance of the firms and the firms' goals regarding export program. Goals of those firms that perceived their performance as above average become more committed toward expansion than the average performance firms. The above average firms tend to be more aggressive toward expanding export programs, whereas the average firms are more conservative.

Section B of table 4.3 shows that high and low export sales groups were significantly different (at 5% level) with regard to the firms' export program goals. Data in this section show that 80 percent of firms in the high export sales group (with annual export sales of HK$ 50 million or over) changed their goals toward expansion of export programs. Whereas 54 percent of the low export sales group (with annual export sales below HK$ 50 million) remained unchanged in their goals regarding export program, only 20 percent of the high export sales firms gave the no change response. The ability and willingness to expand the export program are probably important factors in explaining the better performance of most firms in the high export sales group.

The group of firms whose goals regarding export program have become more committed toward expansion over the past four years and the group whose goals have remained practically the same were found to be significantly different (at 1% level) in terms of their emphasis on distribution channels. Section C of table 4.3 shows that 79 percent of the firms with goals committed toward expanding their export programs placed greater emphasis (a rating of highly important) on distribution channel strategy than firms having goals that aimed to maintain status quo. Meanwhile, as many as 67 percent of the latter firms and 21 percent of the former firms placed limited emphasis (a rating of important) on distribution. This is consistent with the premise that the export program goals are important determinants in the formulation of export channel strategy.

The foregoing analysis leads us to conclude that there is statistical evidence to support Hypothesis 1. This shows that goals of firms with higher volume of exports are more committed towards expansion in their export programs. In addition, firms with goals committed toward expanding their export programs tend to place greater emphasis on distribution channel strategy.

After accepting Hypothesis 1, it will be useful to find out whether the proportion of export channel functions performed by the firms differs with respect to different levels of concern placed on foreign competition and trade restrictions in importing countries.

The data in section A of table 4.4 show a highly significant association (at 1% level) between different levels of concern placed by the firms on foreign competition and the proportion of export channel functions performed by the firms. Eighty-two percent of the firms that were more concerned about foreign competition (with a rating of over 25 points) performed an increased proportion of export channel functions, whereas 67 percent of the less concerned firms (with a rating of zero to 25 points) performed the same proportion. Responding to increased competition from South Korea and Taiwan, the Hong Kong manufacturing firms can improve their competitive edge by providing additional services or incentives for channel agencies or institutions in the existing export channel structures, such as financing inventory and promotional programs.

Likewise, the data in section B show that firms which were more concerned about quotas and tariffs (with a rating of over 25 points) and firms which were less concerned (with a rating of zero to 25 points) are significantly different (at 10% level) in terms of proportion of export channel functions performed. The more concerned firms performed an increased proportion of channel functions as evidenced by 80 percent of the more concerned firms absorbing channel functions from existing channel intermediaries. However, 50 percent of the less concerned firms maintained the same proportion and the other half performed an increased proportion of functions in the distribution channel. The extent that trade restrictions can affect individual manufacturer in the clothing industry depends on the allocation of quotas. Will the manufacturer have sufficient quotas to export his orders? Will he need additional quotas from the transfer market? Although the cost of buying quotas can be included in the export prices, there are times that clothing manufacturers are not able to obtain (through allocation or purchase) sufficient quotas to export all orders. The electronics industry faces mainly tariffs imposed by importing countries, which are often included in the prices of exports or the importers are responsible for paying the tariffs.

The preceding analysis suggests that those Hong Kong manufacturers that are more concerned about foreign competition and trade restrictions tend to perform an increased proportion of export channel functions than those less concerned firms. There is consistent evidence to support Hypothesis 2, which shows that the larger and more successful Hong Kong manufacturing firms are responding to increases in overseas competition and trade restrictions in importing countries by performing an increased proportion of export channel functions for intermediaries in the existing export channel structures.

Selection of Export Distribution Channels

One of the objectives of the book is to answer the following questions: (1) How is the export distribution channel selected by the Hong Kong manufacturing firms? (2) What factors affect the choice of an appropriate export distribution channel? The purpose of these questions is to determine how manufacturers would select their export distribution channels.

To begin, the amount of time the executive in charge of export operations spends on export matters varied between the initial and the current years of export operations. As shown in table 4.5, only 38 and 71 percent of the executives in clothing and electronics firms respectively worked full-time on export matters during the initial years. The remaining executives were all working on export matters on a part-time basis. However, during the current years of export operations, 88 percent of the clothing firms and 100 percent of the electronics firms indicated the employment of full-time executives in charge of export matters. The increase in employment of full-time executives handling export matters suggests the increase in allocation of management time for channel decisions. As discussion in earlier sections of this chapter has shown, more emphasis is placed on distribution with expansion in export programs of the firms.

Figure 4.1 shows the structure of several alternative export distribution channels selected by Hong Kong manufacturing firms during the initial and the current years of export operations. The manufacturing firms could rely on Hong Kong-based resident buyers, export buying agents, export merchants or agents to handle their export functions; establish their own export departments; contact foreign based agents or merchants directly; or set up their own sales offices or branches in export markets, which represents the most direct form of exporting.

During the initial years (first five years), as reported in table 4.6, 63 percent of the clothing firms sold their products to Hong Kong-based resident buyers and 59 percent indicated the use of Hong Kong-based export merchants. Hong Kong-based export agents were employed by 44 percent of the clothing firms and 31 percent relied on the service of Hong Kong-based export buying agents. Only 69 percent of the clothing firms had established their own export departments. Foreign-based agents were used by 19 percent of the clothing firms and 13 percent reported using foreign based merchants. None of the 32 clothing firms responding to the questionnaire indicated the establishment of sales offices or branches in export markets.

For the electronics industry, 71 percent of the firms sold their output directly to Hong Kong-based resident buyers during the initial years of export operations. Twenty-nine percent of the firms reported using Hong Kong-based export merchants, and Hong Kong-based export agents were used by the same percentage of electronics firms. Fourteen percent of the firms sold their products to Hong Kong-based export buying agents, while 71 percent of the electronics firms had their own export departments. Each of the foreign-based agent and foreign-based merchant categories was used by 14 percent of the firms, and two of the electronics firms responding to the questionnaire had set up sales offices or branches in export markets.

Comparing the export channel structure in the initial years to the current years (current five years), there was a significant rise in the use of Hong Kong-based resident buyers by the clothing industry. Other structural changes in export channels of the clothing industry included the reduction in usage of Hong Kong-based export merchants from 59 to 56 percent. Both the uses of Hong Kong-based export agents and Hong Kong-based export buying agents increased by approximately six percent. Eighty-eight percent of the clothing firms reported having their own export departments, an increase of 19 percent over the 69 percent during the initial years of export operations. The use of foreign-based agents and foreign-based merchants registered increases of 12 and 24 percent respectively. Thirty-one percent of the clothing firms had set up their own sales offices or branches in foreign markets.

The export channel structure of the electronics industry during the current years of export operations showed no changes regarding Hong Kong-based resident buyers, export buying agents, and export agents. The use of Hong Kong-based export merchants increased from 29 to 44 percent. All 14 (or 100 percent) of the electronics firms reported the operations of their own export departments in handling export matters. The categories of foreign-based agents, foreign based-merchants, and foreign sales offices or branches of the firms showed increases of 15, 15 and 43 percent respectively.

Three observations may be made. First, the use of multiple channels is very common among Hong Kong manufacturing firms. Instead of relying on one type of intermediary in the export distribution channel, the manufacturing firms are utilizing the services provided by a combination of Hong Kong-based and/or foreign-based channel agencies and institutions. Second, there are notable variations among industries in terms of their reliance on outside channel agencies or institutions to perform a portion of the firms' channel functions. Looking at the channel structure during the current years of export operations, 100 percent of the electronics firms had established their own export departments as compared to 88 percent for the clothing firms. In addition, 57 percent of the electronics firms owned foreign sales offices or branches compared to only 31 percent for the clothing firms. Finally, there exists a trend of moving toward direct exporting in both the clothing and electronics industries. Firms in these two industries increasingly perform the bulk of their export channel functions themselves through their export departments, export managers, or sales offices or branches in foreign markets.

According to table 4.7, 31 percent of the clothing firms and 57 percent of the electronics firms had established sales offices or branches in foreign markets, with the majority located in the United States, West Germany, and United Kingdom. At the same time, 27 and 50 percent of the remaining firms in clothing and electronics respectively reported plans to set up sales offices or branches in the coming five years. The most important reason for setting up sales offices or branches abroad cited by clothing executives is the fear of major market countries shifting to import quotas instead of the present export quota system administered by the Hong Kong government. With the establishment of sales offices or branches in major market countries, the Hong Kong manufacturers will be classified as importers and be included in the allocation of import quotas when they become effective. Executives from electronics firms mentioned the need to provide better customer service in foreign markets as the key motive behind the establishment of sales offices or branches in foreign markets.

Besides the overall structural profile of export channels discussed above, it is instructive to take note of the number of alternative channels considered by the firms before selecting the export distribution channel. The data in table 4.8 suggest that 38 percent of the clothing firms and 14 percent of the electronics firms considered two to three alternative channels during the initial years of export operations. Another 50 percent of the clothing firms and 71 percent of the electronics firms considered four to five alternatives; and 12 and 14 percent of clothing and electronics firms respectively considered over five alternative channels. The percentages changed drastically during the current years of export operations; 12 percent of the clothing firms considered only two or three alternatives; 50 percent of the clothing firms and 57 percent of the electronics firms considered four to five alternatives; and the percentage of firms considering over five alternative channels increased to 38 and 43 percent for the clothing and the electronics firms respectively. This tendency of considering a large number of alternative channels reflects the firms' increasing allocation of management time for export matters and the greater emphasis placed on distribution channel strategy as a result of expansion in export programs.

Table 4.9 indicates the management's responses and views pertaining to the criteria used by Hong Kong manufacturing firms in selecting export distribution channels. For the clothing industry, market area served was the most frequently used criterion, as evidenced by 69 and 81 percent of the firms using it during the initial and the current years of export operations respectively. Market potential ranked second with 63 percent of the firms reporting its use during the initial and the current years. Experience was used by 50 percent of the firms during the initial years and 69 percent of the firms during the current years of export operations. Financial strength was used as a criterion for selecting channel by 25 and 56 percent of the firms during the initial and the current years respectively. None of the clothing firms reported using growth plan as a selection criterion during the initial years, and only 13 percent of the firms used it during the current years.

Looking at the electronics industry, market potential was ranked as the most frequently used selection criterion with 86 percent of the firms using it during the initial and the current years of export operations. Market area served and financial strength tied for second place during the current years of export operations, representing increased of 43 and 15 percent respectively when compared to their uses during the initial years. Experience as a channel selection criterion increased from its usage by 29 percent of the firms during the initial years to 43 percent during the current years. Growth plan was not used at all by the electronics firms during the initial or the current years of export operations.

By comparing the data according to industries, certain differences are noted. First, the clothing firms perceive market area served to be more important in selecting export channel, whereas the electronics firms believe market potential is more important. Second, growth plan is only considered by clothing firms during the current years of export operations. Third, financial strength is the criterion registering the largest increase in usage by the clothing firms, from 25 percent in the initial years to 56 percent in the current years, whereas market area served increases from 14 to 57 percent in its usage by the electronics firms. These differences illustrate the emphasis and concern of the two industries in selecting export distribution channels.

In addition, when the five selective criteria are compared, every criterion except one shows an increase in its usage by manufacturing firms in selecting export distribution channels. The only exception is market potential, which remains unchanged in terms of its usage by clothing and electronics firms during the initial and the current years of export operations.

The difference in terms of the stages of development between the clothing and the electronics industries is the key reason in explaining the differences and shifts in usage of criteria for selecting export distribution channels. The rapid increase in usage of market area served by electronics firms suggests that the electronics industry, the younger of the two industries under investigation, is gradually following the practices of the clothing industry.

Evaluation and Modification of Export Distribution Channels

It is frequently suggested that the larger and more successful firms are likely to perform evaluations on a more regular basis and make modifications in export channels as a result of strategic marketing planning. Therefore, it is important to ascertain the extent to which clothing and electronics firms show differences in degrees of management involvement, frequency of time spent and criteria used in channel evaluation. Moreover, it is necessary to explore the perceived performance of channel agencies or institutions by the firms and other events which have led to modification of the export distribution channels.

Who are the executives involved in evaluating the performance of the export distribution channels? According to table 4.10, 94 and 86 percent of the clothing and electronics firms respectively reported the involvement of top management in the evaluation of export channels. This is consistent with the premise that there has been increasing emphasis and greater control from high levels of authority within the firms on export distribution channels. The involvement of sales executives in evaluating the export channels was reported by 44 percent of the clothing firms and 29 percent of the electronics firms. Marketing executives were involved in 19 percent of the clothing firms and 29 percent of the electronics firms. For several surveyed firms, sales was viewed as an early form of marketing. Production executives were mentioned by 31 and 14 percent of clothing and electronics firms respectively. The involvement of accounting executives was reported only in the electronics industry by 14 percent of the firms, whereas the involvement of finance executives was indicated by six percent of the clothing firms only.

Next, let us turn to comparisons between the two industries regarding the frequency of evaluation in export channels (table 4.11). The electronics firms tended to perform more frequent evaluations (monthly, quarterly, or semi-annually) as reported by 79 percent of the firms, whereas only 44 percent of the clothing firms performed more frequent channel evaluation. The corresponding percentages for firms that performed evaluations less frequently (annually or above) were 56 and 21 percent of the clothing and electronics firms respectively.

Section B of table 4.11 indicates the amount of time spent each year by the manufacturing firms in evaluating the export channels. When the two industries were compared, 71 percent of the electronics firms reported that a substantial amount of time (a rating of 3 through 5 on a scale of 1 to 5) was spent in evaluating the export channels, whereas only 34 percent of the clothing firms reported the same response. About 29 percent of the electronics firms indicated that a minimal amount of time (a rating of 1 and 2 on a scale of 1 to 5) was spent on channel evaluation. Sixty-six percent of the clothing firms reported spending a minimal amount of time on channel evaluation. One of the executives interviewed suggested that because of the current development of the electronics industry, most top executives in electronics firms are professionally trained managers. With the long history of the clothing industry, top executives of most clothing firms are self-taught entrepreneurs. The background of top executives probably affects their outlooks on channel evaluation, which is an important factor in explaining the different emphasis placed on frequency and duration of channel evaluation by the clothing and the electronics industries.

Having ascertained the frequency and duration of channel evaluation, it will be useful to find out if the two industries differ in the criteria used in evaluating the performance of export distribution channels. The figures in table 4.12 reflect certain differences between clothing and electronics firms in their uses of evaluative criteria. Whereas the clothing firms rated sales and gross margin as the two most frequently used criteria (by 69 pecent of the firms) in evaluating the export distribution channels, the electronics firms preferred cost and market share, with 71 percent of the firms using each in their channel evaluation. In the clothing industry, the next frequently used criterion was cost, as 63 percent of the firms reported using it. Market share and investment followed with 56 and 25 percent of the firms using them respectively. As for the electronics industry, sales was the next frequently used evaluative criterion as reported by 43 percent of the firms, and gross margin and investment tied for fourth place with 29 percent of the firms separately reported their uses.

In this analysis, responses regarding criteria for evaluating the performance of the export distribution channels were examined. What events led to a modification of the export distribution channels and in what respects do clothing and electronics firms differ?

Let us begin with an analysis of the respondents' perception of performance of channel agencies or institutions, which are often believed to cause channel modification. The results of comparisons regarding performance of intermediaries in the two industries are shown in table 4.13. Performance of intermediaries of clothing firms was perceived to be satisfactory by over 69 percent of the firms in all four attributes: cooperativeness, dependability, intelligence, and competence. Performance of intermediaries of electronics firms was rated satisfactory by 86 percent of the firms in the attributes of intelligence and competence, and by 57 percent of the firms in the attributes of cooperativeness and dependability. Only a small percentage of firms from the two industries rated themselves as "highly satisfied" with their intermediaries in these attributes. Over 13 percent of the clothing firms separately reported dissatisfaction regarding their intermediaries' performance over all four of the attributes, with lack of dependability cited as "dissatisfied" by the largest number of firms. Likewise, dependability was the attribute cited most frequently as dissatisfactory by firms in the electronics industry. Dissatisfaction in cooperativeness and in competence were also reported respectively by 29 and 14 percent of the electronics firms.

One of the executives interviewed mentioned that the lack of dependability of channel intermediaries is one of the major problems in export distribution channels; it triggers firms to set up sales offices abroad to deal directly with overseas buyers. Dissatisfaction in performance of channel agencies or institutions tends to bring about changes and modification in export distribution channels toward the direction of direct exporting. According to the interview reports, dependability was the attribute most clothing and electronics executives rated as dissatisfactory.

Turning to other events that have led to modification of the export distribution channels, table 4.14 shows that changes in demand and customer needs tied for the top position as the most frequently mentioned events leading to channel modification in the clothing industry, whereas the top places in the electronics industry went to new markets and changes in demand. Over 40 percent of the clothing firms reported that competition and new markets have led to modification in the export channels, and 43 percent of the electronics firms indicated the same impact for competition and customer needs. These results are supported by many remarks made by executives during in-depth interviews. Product changes, changes in sales, changes in profitability, loss of market share, and changes in costs were frequently cited by clothing and electronics firms as important events leading to channel modification in export distribution. The survey responses indicate that the most frequently mentioned events reported by clothing firms are virtually identical with those cited by electronics firms. In other words, executives in the two industries appear to be in complete agreement regarding the important events behind channel modification.

The questionnaire results suggest that the Hong Kong manufacturing firms utilized different sets of criteria in their selection and evaluation of the export distribution channels, and the interview reports supported the same findings. However, the firms participating in the interview process had not shown much progress toward designing a distribution channel system to have formalized criteria for use in channel design. Channel selection, evlauation and modification took place as different tasks of managing the export channel. There was a lack of overall planning along the line of strategic marketing planning. Most of the firms were involved in planning, but there was no evidence to suggest that these firms based their export channel strategies upon carefully developed strategic marketing plans. In fact, very few of the firms have mastered the systematic development of strategic marketing plans.

Channel Involvement, Channel Evaluation and Firm Characteristics

In order to gain more insight into the factors which influence the degree of channel involvement, the final phase of the analysis involves an investigation of relationships between channel involvement, channel evaluation and specific characteristics of the firms. By cross-tablulating relevant responses of the questionnaire, the significance of relationships is tested using the chi-square analysis.

Channel Involvement and Characteristics of the Firms

Characteristics of the firms which are particularly relevant include ownership, export experience (as measured by number of years in exporting), export sales growth, average annual export sales, and size of operations (as measured by number of workers).

The degree by channel involvement of each firm is classified into high- and low-involvement groups according to its channel structure during the current years of export operations. The high-involvement group includes firms that have their own export departments and use foreign channel agents and/or merchants, and/or have set up sales offices or branches in export markets. The low-involvement firms are those that basically rely on Hong Kong-based channel agents and/or merchants; they may or may not have their own export departments.

Section A of table 4.15 shows no evidence that high channel involvement firms are more associated with private ownership than are low channel involvement firms. Both high- and low-involvement firms are distributed rather similarly between private- and public-owned firms. Therefore, one cannot conclude that high- and low-involvement groups are significantly different in terms of ownership status.

Similarly, no significant association between degree of channel involvement and export experience can be found from data in Section B. Firms with different years of export experience are proportionately represented in high- and low-involvement groups. For those firms with less than 10 years of export experience, there were 12 high-involvement firms and 10 low-involvement firms, whereas firms with 10 or more years of export experience included 16 and 8 high- and low-involvement firms respectively.

Likewise, export sales growth shows no significant relationship between high- and low-involvement groups. Section C of table 4.15 shows 50 percent of the high-involvement firms reported an export growth rate of under 10 percent and the other half indicated 10 percent or above export growth. Although differences exist in the proportion of high or low growth rate for low-involvement firms, the chi-square of 1.409 (with one degree of freedom) is not large enough to be statistically significant.

Looking at the relationship between degree of channel involvement and average annual export sales, the chi-square of 4.108 (with one degree of freedom) is statistically significant at the 5 percent level. Section D shows higher average annual export sales for high-involvement firms. In percentages, 57 percent of the high-involvement firms reported average annual export sales HK$ 50 million or above, whereas only 22 percent of the low-involvement firms managed to achieve such a high export sales level.

Finally, high- and low-involvement groups were found to be significantly different in terms of their size of operations. Data in Section E of table 4.16 indicate that high channel involvement firms are mostly larger-sized firms (with 200 workers or more) and low channel involvement firms are likely to be smaller (below 200 workers). The chi-square of 4.221 (with one degree of freedom) is significant at the five percent level, which provides statistical evidence that the degree of channel involvement tends to go up with size of the firms.

The preceding analysis suggests that high- and low-involvement firms are roughly the same with regard to ownership, export experience, and export sales growth. However, the high channel involvement firms tend to be larger in size and more successful in export sales relative to the low channel involvement firms. There is little doubt that the advantages gained through the economics of scale accrue from larger size of operation, together with the higher volume of export sales are important requirements for manufacturing firms in moving toward high channel involvement. In addition, success tends to build on itself, the more successful firms often generate better export performance than the "average" firms.

Channel Evaluation and Characteristics of the Firms

An analysis of the association between frequency of channel evaluations and characteristics of the firms which have direct influence on export performance can provide further insight into the factors influencing channel involvement. Relevant characteristics of the firms include export growth rate, average annual export sales, and size of operations.

As Section A of table 4.16 indicates, no significant differences were found regarding frequency of channel evaluation and export sales growth. However, significant differences appeared when frequency of channel evaluation was cross-tabulated with average annual export sales. Section B shows that 80 percent of the firms with export sales of HK$ 50 million or over reported more frequent evaluation, whereas only 35 percent of the firms with export sales under HK$ 50 million performed more frequent channel evaluation. The firms with higher average annual export sales tended to perform more frequent channel evaluation than did firms with lower average annual export sales.

The larger- and smaller-sized firms were also found to show significant differences with regard to frequency of evaluation. Data in Section C indicate the larger-sized firms performed more frequent export channel evaluations than smaller-sized firms. With over two-thirds of the larger-sized firms performing more frequent channel evaluation, only 31 percent of the smaller-sized firms reported the same response. Meanwhile, 69 percent of the smaller-sized firms and less than one-third of the larger-sized firms performed evaluation in the export distribution channel on a less frequent basis. One executive interviewed suggested that most larger-sized firms are managed by business executives who show a high degree of sophistication in export management. Such sophistication has probably led them to continuously evaluate the performance of the export distribution channel.

Channel Evaluation and Channel Involvement

Looking at the third hypothesis of the study, which is re-stated as follows:

Hypothesis 3:   Based upon evaluation conducted on a regular basis, the larger and more successful Hong Kong manufacturing firms will attempt to seek greater control over their export distribution channels by changing the export channel structures toward more direct exporting and less delegating through indirect exporting.

What can we say about the relationship between channel evaluation and channel involvement? Table 4.17 shows the association between frequency of channel evaluation and degree of channel involvement.

The firms that performed channel evaluations on a more frequent basis tended to be more involved in performing the export channel functions relative to firms that reported less frequent channel evaluations. Whereas 84 percent of the firms that performed more frequent channel evaluations reported a high degree of channel involvement, only 33 percent of those firms that performed less frequent evaluations responded likewise. The chi-square test shows a value of 10.265 (with one degree of freedom), which is highly significant at the 1 percent level. The ability to seek and monitor export opportunities as a result of frequent channel evaluation is probably an important factor in explaining the movement toward direct exporting of the high-involvement group.

The final part of the analysis leads us to conclude that there is consistent evidence to support Hypothesis 3. It shows that based upon channel evaluation conducted on a regular basis, the larger and more successful Hong Kong manufacturing firms are seeking greater control over their export distribution channels through a higher degree of channel involvement. The firms are changing their export channel structures toward more direct exporting and less delegating through indirect exporting.

5

Conclusions

This chapter summarizes the conclusions of this book. The implications of the findings for business managers, academicians, and government officials are also discussed. Finally, the chapter concludes with a section concerning suggestions for future research.

The purpose of the book is to gain insights into how managers devise strategies and make decisions for domestic manufacturing firms in export distribution channels. The book poses three central questions. First, how is the export distribution channel selected by the Hong Kong manufacturing firms and what factors affect the choice of an appropriate export distribution channel? Second, do the manufacturing firms in Hong Kong make structural and operational modifications in their export channel strategies to accommodate changes associated with expansion in export markets? Third, what specific criteria are used to evaluate the export distribution channel? How often is the export channel evaluated? Who is involved in the evaluation?

An extensive review of the literature was undertaken to assess previous evidence on export distribution channels. The literature search was also used to prepare the questionnaire and interview guide for the field research phase of the study. Three conclusions were drawn from examination of the literature. First, the large body of literature in distribution channels addresses channels of distribution in a domestic context. Second, the few pieces of literature that discuss distribution channels in an international context have been directed toward the multinational firms. There is a large gap in the literature in the area of domestic firms engaging in international operations through exporting. Finally, there is a complete lack of empirical studies on export distribution channels of Hong Kong manufacturing firms.

The study has employed two research approaches to examine export channel strategy for Hong Kong manufacturing firms. The first approach was a questionnaire survey of 200 Hong Kong manufacturing firms from the two leading industries, clothing and electronics. The structured questionnaire was sent to export managers or managers involved in day-to-day export operations. Analysis of data from the questionnaire provided the basis for a cross-sectional analysis of export channel strategy in the two industries. The second approach was an in-depth interview with ten firms selected from respondents of the questionnaire survey. The interviews used open-ended questions to allow top level executives to express their views and experience relating to strategy in export distribution channels.

Summary of Important Conclusions

The two Hong Kong industries under investigation, clothing and electronics, have undergone drastic changes in their growth and development since their beginning stages. Both have survived ups and downs in their export operations and become the first and second place industries in terms of export earnings for Hong Kong.

The clothing industry enjoys the number one spot in terms of export sales, number of establishments, and employment of manufacturing workforce in Hong Kong. Despite the import restrictions from major export markets and intensified competition from South Korea and Taiwan, the outlook for Hong Kong clothing exports continues to be good. As increasing numbers of Hong Kong clothing manufacturers are switching from producing low priced items to high quality high priced, fashionable clothing, Hong Kong is rapidly shedding the cheap product image of its clothing exports. There is also growing acceptance of the quality of higher priced Hong Kong clothing.

Looking at the electronics industry, the second largest manufacturing industry in Hong Kong, it has evolved during the last two decades from assembling simple transistor radios to producing high quality and sophisticated products. The outlook for the industry continues to show improvement. The electronics industry has been growing mainly because of Hong Kong manufacturers' advancement in technology and the trend of developing and producing high quality products. However, the rapidly increasing wage rate and material costs will result in less spectacular growth going into the '80s.

Analysis of the survey findings supported the first exploratory proposition discussed at the beginning of this book. The Hong Kong manufacturing firms selected as samples in this study represented the larger and more successful firms. Most of these firms formulated their channel strategies for export distribution with consideration of company goals as well as important forces in the international environment.

In terms of Hypothesis 1, volume of export sales was found to have a strong relationship with changes in company goals. The goals of the firms regarding export programs often changed toward expansion as the volume of exports increased. At the same time, company goals were also found to be associated significantly with the emphasis firms placed on distribution channels. Firms with goals committed toward expanding their export programs tended to place greater emphasis on distribution channel strategy. The clothing and the electronics firms were remarkably similar in this respect.

Hypothesis 2 was also confirmed by analysis of the findings. The proportion of export channel functions performed by the firms was significantly different with regard to different levels of concern placed by the firms on overseas competition and trade restrictions. Hong Kong manufacturing firms were found to be performing an increased proportion of export channel functions for existing channel intermediaries as a response to increases in overseas competition and trade restriction. However, firms in the clothing industry perceived a more important role for trade restrictions, whereas the electronics firms were more concerned about foreign competition.

The increased importance of the export distribution channels was evidenced by the increased participation of full-time executives in handling export matters, especially in the selection, evaluation and modification of export channels.

The structure of the export distribution channels varied between the initial and the current years of export operations. Hong Kong-based channel intermediaries were used extensively during the initial years of exporting. However, as the firms developed experience in exporting, they were found to be increasingly reliant on foreign-based agencies or institutions to handle some of their export functions. At the same time, organizational changes were taking place, resulting in establishment of export departments to handle export functions separately from other functional areas of the firms. During the current years of export operations, firms in the two industries were found increasingly to be performing the bulk of export channel functions through the use of sales offices or branches in foreign markets. Evidence also suggested that Hong Kong manufacturing firms frequently utilized multiple channels to expand their market opportunities. Firms in the electronics industry tended to be more aggressive in moving towards direct exporting than the clothing firms.

In selecting the appropriate export channels, there existed a tendency among the firms to consider a larger number of alternative channels. With regard to criteria used in selecting export channels, views of firms in the two industries converged appreciably despite differences with regard to a few aspects. In addition, most criteria were found to be used frequently by firms in selecting their export channels.

Although differences dominated the analysis of the involvement of types of executives in evaluating export distribution channels, there was similarity among the clothing and the electronics firms with regard to the heavy involvement of top management in channel evaluation. In connection with the criteria used in evaluating export channel performance, several important differences were revealed. For example, whereas the clothing firms used sales and investment most frequently as criteria in evaluating export channel performance, the electronics firms preferred to use cost and market share most frequently.

There was little difference between clothing and electronics firms regarding their appraisal of performance of channel agencies or institutions.

Most firms in the two industries gave similar dissatisfactory ratings to the attribute of dependability for their intermediaries. Concerning events leading to export channel modification, executives in the two industries were practically in complete agreement about their selection of the top four most frequently mentioned events. The order of other frequently mentioned events was not significantly different.

The findings of the analysis provided no evidence to conclude that export channel strategy was based upon carefully developed strategic marketing plans of the firms. Channel selection, evaluation and modification took place as different tasks of managing the export channel, they were not related to an overall strategic marketing plan. There was very little evidence of systematic development of strategic marketing planning among firms participating in the in-depth interview process.

The final phase of the analysis examined relationships between channel involvement, channel evaluation, and specific characteristics of the firms. Hypothesis 3 was tested to determine the degree of channel involement with different frequencies of channel evaluation.

There was no evidence to show association between degree of channel involvement and ownership status. Likewise, export experience and export sales growth showed no significant relationships with high- and low-involvement firms. However, high channel involvement firms reported higher average annual export sales and employed larger number of workers relative to low channel involvement firms.

No significant differences were found regarding frequency of channel evaluation and export sales growth. However, firms with higher average annual export sales and larger size of operations tended to perform more frequent evaluation in the export distribution channels.

In terms of Hypothesis 3, it was generally supported. The frequency of channel evaluation was found to have a strong relationship with degree of channel involvement. The firms that performed channel evaluation on a more frequent basis tended to be seeking greater control over their export distribution channels through greater degree of channel involvement.

Implications of the Study

The study has a number of implications for business managers, academicians, and government officials. The broad implication for doing research in the developing countries relates to insights provided by the empirical method used in studying export distribution channel. Although this study is exploratory in nature, it should contribute to the development of more rigorous methodology for researching export distribution channels in the developing countries.

Since only larger and more successful Hong Kong manufacturing firms in clothing and electronics were included in the sample, the findings of this research should benefit those less successful firms in Hong Kong as well as those presently considering exporting to foreign markets. This study has pointed out the importance of effective channel strategy in export distribution. In addition, the descriptive and analytical aspects of the study also provide insights into the profile of export distribution strategies in Hong Kong's clothing and electronics industries and some of the relationships between decision areas in export distribution channels.

Placing greater emphasis on the export distribution channels requires additional commitment of the firms' resources. First, human resources in terms of top management time and capable managerial talents to capitalize on strategic opportunities and successfully resolve problems in export channels are needed. Second, many strategic opportunities can be capitalized only through heavy financial investment. Financial resources must be available when the firms want to perform an increased proportion of the export channel functions. If expansions in export programs are to be successful, the firms must be prepared to invest additional resources.

Domestic- or foreign-based channel agencies and institutions provide means of performing export channel functions for the manufacturing firms. However, the selection and management of channel intermediaries necessitates expenditure of resources. The involvement of top management is frequently required in the selection, evaluation and control of channel intermediaries. Effective evaluation and control process is dependent upon the ability of management to measure performance and to make adjustments in the export distribution channel. Use of domestic intermediaries is common during the initial phase of export operations, and foreign intermediaries are increasingly relied upon as the firms move toward direct exporting.

In addition, it is important to develop an adequate information base for decision making in the export distribution channels, such as screening and evaluation of foreign-based channel intermediaries and market opportunities. This would suggest the development of data banks and foreign market research and indicates a need for govnernment cooperation. In fact, the Hong Kong Trade Development Council is fulfilling its mission by performing activities along this line.[1] Academicians and policy makers in developing countries interested in stimulating exports need to get themselves involved in educating business managers in the areas of export channel management and international market research. It is generally recognized that exports of many developing countries may be held back by a shortage of capable managers. The appropriate policy would be to invest in human capital by giving intensive training in specific areas of export management, for example, export marketing management.

Suggestion for Planning the Export Distribution Channels[2]

As the research findings demonstrate, strategic planning is a useful approach to the analysis of problems and managerial decision making in export distribution channels. Some reasons for the logical extension of strategic thinking to export distribution channels are as follows:

1. Channel relationships between manufacturers and intermediaries are evolving as manufacturers seek access to new markets, strategic planning is the logical method for translating the manufacturers' objectives into performance results.
2. Most approaches to strategic planning also emphasize the analysis of expected changes in political or legal constraints and their likely impact on the company in its market. Companies engaged in export marketing must keep abreast of developments and changes in export distribution channel regulations, such as custom tariffs, quotas, import valuation methods, inspection procedures, and packing and marking rules.
3. Strategic planning is of crucial importance in export distribution channels as a means of relating desired performance results with alternative designs of channel structures.

Strategic planning is best described by a dynamic model of a cyclically repeated process of sequential research inquiries and managerial decisions for the purpose of achieving desired results. The field research and review of the strategic planning literature (Sultan, et al, 1972; Schoeffler, et al, 1974; Buzzell, et al, 1975; Paul, et al, 1978; and Holloway and King, 1979) suggest the following steps in the planning of export distribution channels:

1. Preliminary statement of objectives or mission.
2. Analysis of export markets, overseas customers, and technologies.
3. Analysis of export channel structure and alternatives.
4. Examination of the macroeconomic and political environment.
5. Analysis of the competition.
6. Assessment of the company's internal resources.
7. Development and formulation of export channel strategies.
8. Export distribution channel evaluation and control.

There is nothing sacrosanct in the eight steps of the planning process, this is merely an effort to include the most important steps in a logical order.

The first step, a preliminary statement of objectives or mission, for many firms this will be a reevaluation of their basic business purposes. Most planners agree that this kind of review of basic aims needs to be carried out at least once a year. All too often, the multiplicity of products and export market differences cause confusion. Without a clear concept of the basic purposes, the manager is likely to make serious mistakes in export channel design and management decisions. The export distribution channel is a vital linkage or support system between manufacturer and final buyer, and the basic objectives will define the kinds of support functions or linkage strategies that will be most effective in serving customers in different economic, political and competitive environments.

Analysis in the strategic process begins with export markets and overseas customers. Export market analysis refers to the number of customers in a given export market or market segments, the growth rates, the seasonality or cyclical nature of sales in different markets, and the sensitivity of customers to changes in export marketing variables, especially in the export distribution channel. Overseas customer analysis include current and future shift in produce usage behavior, service needs, reasons for buying, ability and willingness to pay more, as well as demographic changes. Export distribution channel strategy can depend on accurate reading of the current and good forecasts of any or all of these variables.

The analysis of technology is also very important in strategic planning for export distribution channels. The computer revolution in export channel communication and control is getting notice, with a large potential to be realized. Similar advantages have been realized by international marketing companies through multimode physical distribution. As logistics develop into a highly expert and specialized function in the firm, strategic planning will be more able to understand the competitive implications of technological change and assess the advantage of implementing new techniques.

At this stage of the planning process, the firm is ready to take a close look at the export distribution channel. The firm should begin with a diagramatic view of the structure of export distribution channel system so as to understand the relative positions and linkages among the different channel members. Some knowledge of the kinds of functions performed at each level of the export channel is also needed. Seven basic functions are performed in the export distribution channel: financing, inventory, advertising, sales, physical distribution, service, and information gathering about overseas customers and competitors. These functions are the dynamic of the export distribution channel, facilitating and expediting the physical and legal flows of goods. The analysis should focus on the weak links or functions which are not being executed effectively, as well as the strengths of the export channel system.

An examination of the macroeconomic and political environment can provide understanding of trends for the future and impacts of governmental constraints. This analysis is highly important to the exporting firms which needs to keep abreast of market growth, inflation, prospects for political instability, monetary and foreign exchange rate fluctuations and other key indicators in the export markets which it serves. Export channel effectiveness is also greatly affected by changes in customs regulations, tariff and nontariff barriers. The increase in protectionism since the late 1970s has caused massive shifts in strategy by companies trying to find ways of overcoming the rising barriers to trade.

The firm must determine the approach to competition before deciding on the export channel strategy. Strategy planning should consider an analysis of the competition in finding means to develop competitive advantages. Market share, financial position, consumer franchise, and strategy effectiveness are major variables that are used in competitive evaluations. The firm needs to determine the differences between major competitors and competing products in export markets, so as to effectively react in the market place by developing an ideal marketing mix and export distribution channel strategy to exploit the differences. Continuing anticipation and projection of competitive movements and reactions should lead to new strategies for maintaining and increasing the share of export markets.

In some respects of the process of strategic planning has already examined the internal resources of the firm, but at this stage of planning a detailed and thorough analysis is essential. The emphasis on export distribution channel suggests that the inquiry should focus on channel management, international logistics, and export markets or areas information. Area specialists are needed for different markets or regions. Some of the skills can be hired through contacts with marketing research firms overseas, multinational banks, or export management consulting companies. However, there is an irreducible minimum of human resources needed within the firm, and this part of the planning process should be quite explicit in identifying such needs.

Development and formulation of export channel strategies should fit in with the overall, coordinated management strategy of the firm. The manager should evaluate not only the export distribution channels, but the market segments and the product offerings as well. The key strategic question is: which combination of channels, markets and products would most likely accomplish the company's objectives of profitability?

For example, one manufacturing firm may have high sales levels and market shares in each of its export channels; but in most channels the products are in the maturity stage of their life cycles. This results in channel profits being taken away by new competition that is using a technologically more advanced form of export distribution as well as newer products. In this situation, the operating strategy calls for remedial action to respond to the threats of product and distribution obsolescence. The firm should build on its strength of present strong market and channel position to gain rapid diffusion of newer and better products through up to date distribution technology.

Another example looks at a manufacturing firm with only small market shares, and most of its channels are in several high potential markets. Even though its products are of good quality and distribution technology are as good as the competition, profitability in most of these export channels is low because of trade restrictions imposed by the foreign markets. This scenario is similar to the dilemma of Hong Kong clothing manufacturers currently trying to maintain exports to the United States and other western markets. Since quotas pose an immediate threat to these Hong Kong firms, their response has been to attempt to influence the international negotiations for the reduction of the trade barriers and, at the same time, keep channel services and product quality high.

The final step is evaluation and control of the export distribution channel. As an essential part of strategy analysis and formulation, the relationship between investment and sales revenues needs to be evaluated and controlled. A related, but different issue is the evaluation of total costs and sales revenues in alternative export channels. Just as product or export market alternatives need to be assessed, different channel options must be carefully compared and monitored. Different export channel options are often the basis for improved distribution productivity, more effective access to markets, and better growth in sales and profits.

Suggestions for Future Research

This research investigates the area of export distribution channel which has been overlooked with regard to the application of distribution channel concepts. It represents an initial step to provide insights into decision making and strategy formulation in export distribution channels of selected Hong Kong manufacturing firms. Several research directions are possible in the extension and refinement of this book.

This study was concerned only with channel strategy from the manufacturer's point of view. Additional research should consider channel selection, evaluation and modification by domestic and foreign agencies or institutions in export distribution channels. The Hong Kong manufacturers are selecting domestic and foreign channel intermediaries, but these channel intermediaries are also involved in selecting manufacturing firms they want to represent or do business with.

Since this study included manufacturing firms in the clothing and the electronics industries only, future research of a similar nature should include other key industries of Hong Kong to have a more comprehensive look at variations of export channel strategies among different industries. With a larger and more representative sample, the problem of generalizability would be remedied and more sophisticated statistical analysis could be employed.

A third area of research would be to conduct a comparative study with firms from countries that are following the export-led industrialization growth path, such as South Korea, Taiwan, and Singapore. The purpose of such a study would be to identify similarities and differences in the formulation of export channel strategy among firms in these developing countries. Research into the following questions should provide valuable insights: (1) How do firms in these countries formulate export channel strategies? (2) What are the important factors considered by firms in these countries in selection, evaluation and modification of export distribution channels? and (3) What are the trends and patterns in export channel strategies of firms of these countries?

Finally, a promising possibility involves further research and operationalization of the various aspects of a framework for formulation of export channel strategy. This would require the researcher to establish close working relationships with a few prominent manufacturers. The process of formulation of export channel strategy should be investigated to develop a channel strategy model. Variables to be considered should include company objectives and resources; target markets; the rest of the export marketing mix; the selection, evaluation and control of export channels; current and future changes in export channels structures; and the performance of export channel functions.

Appendix 1

Hong Kong as a Financial Centre[1]

Hong Kong ranks as one of the world's leading international financial centres. Banks and other deposit-taking companies; insurance companies, pension funds, unit trusts and similar operations; foreign exchange and money brokers, stock and commodity brokers — these and other financial organisations combine to present a wide range of financial services to both local and international customers. While the overseas links are particularly strong within Southeast Asia. Hong Kong's position as a bridge in the time difference between Japan and Europe has given the territory a vital role to play in world finance.

But the emergence of Hong Kong as a financial centre has not simply been a matter of geography. The government has continually worked towards developing a favourable environment, with sufficient regulation to ensure, so far as possible, sound business standards and confidence in the institutions but without unnecessary impediments of a bureaucratic or fiscal nature.

In contrast to the international dimension, small local operations such as credit unions, pawnbrokers and moneylenders, all of which are subject to some basic statutory regulation, continue to help meet the needs of Hong Kong people.

Unlike other financial centres, Hong Kong has no central bank. Those functions which might typically be performed by one—such as supervising financial institutions, managing official foreign exchange reserves, or providing banking services to the government—are carried out by the relevant government offices, in conjunction with the government's commercial bankers where appropriate. Since the government has not needed to issue any conventional government debt in recent years because of habitual budget surpluses, and since there are no controls on foreign exchange dealing in Hong Kong, the range of central bank functions that have to be undertaken is narrower than in many other countries.

The financial scene in 1982 was dominated by a crisis of confidence, which broke towards the end of September, stemming principally from concern over

1. From *Hong Kong Annual Report 1983,* (Hong Kong: Government Printer, 1983).

Hong Kong's future. Up until then, financial markets were comparatively steady, and any anxieties on this score muted; but these came to the fore following the visit of the British Prime Minister, the Rt Hon Margaret Thatcher, to China and Hong Kong. The exchange rate of the Hong Kong dollar and stock market prices then declined very sharply. Despite official assurances regarding the future stability and prosperity of Hong Kong, the markets remained weak and unduly susceptible to rumours for the remainder of the year.

The property market was particularly affected by the 1997 issue, at a time when it was anyway experiencing a cyclical downturn. As a result, a number of companies involved in property development found themselves in serious financial difficulty. Their problems, and the decline in property prices, in turn placed some financial institutions under strain. Partly because of this, but sparked by the alleged insolvency of one deposit-taking company for reasons apparently unconnected with Hong Kong's future or the property market, a growing loss of confidence in the deposit-taking company sector as a whole developed in November. Reassurances from major banks and the government helped to restore general confidence in the sector, although a handful of individual companies continued to face difficulties.

Before these developments hit the headlines, the event which perhaps drew the most public attention was a rare bank run. Branches of a local bank came under siege for a couple of days in early September from thousands of nervous depositors following entirely groundless rumours that the bank was connected with a jewelry company—part of whose business involved the issue of gold certificates to the customers recording the comany's holding of physical gold for them—which had suddenly ceased trading. Following reassuring statements from the government and from other banks, the run subsided without having spread and without the bank concerned being forced to close its doors.

Monetary Sector

During 1982, a further nine banking licences were granted, bringing the number of licensed banks to 131, of which 35 are local companies. The banks maintain a total of 1,474 offices in Hong Kong. In addition there are 115 representative offices of foreign banks.

Absolute discretion in the granting of banking licences rests with the Governor-in-Council, in accordance with the provisions of the Banking Ordinance. However, certain guiding criteria are applied. Currently, a bank incorporated outside Hong Kong which wishes to apply for a banking licence is required to show total assets (net of contra items) of at least US$12,000 million (this figure is reviewed annually), and its country of incorporation must apply an adequate form of prudential supervision and offer some acceptable form of reciprocity to Hong Kong banks. In addition, the Governor-in-Council will have regard to the number of banks from the applicant's country of incorporation which already hold licences, and to the state of Hong Kong's commercial relations with that country.

A domestic company (one incorporated in Hong Kong and predominantly beneficially owned by Hong Kong interests) must satisfy a separate set of criteria in order to be considered for a banking licence: it must have a paid-up capital of at least $100 million; it must have been in the business of taking deposits from and granting credit to the public for at least 10 years; and it must hold deposits from the public of at least $1,750 million and have total assets of at least $2,500 million (these minima are also reviewed annually).

Banks may accept deposits from the public of any size and any maturity, but the interest rate rules of the Hong Kong Association of Banks result in the setting of maximum rates payable for maturities up to and including one year. However, with effect from March 1982, no limits apply on individual deposits in excess of $500,000 of less than three months term to maturity.

Apart from banks, no company may take deposits from the public unless licensed or registered under the Deposit-taking Companies Ordinance. Licensed status, which is granted at the discretion of the Financial Secretary, is reserved for larger companies which have a minimum issued share capital of $100 million and paid-up capital of $75 million, and which meet certain partially subjective criteria regarding size, ownership and quality of management. Licensed deposit-taking companies may take deposits from the public of any maturity, but in amounts of not less than $500,000. Since the status of licensed deposit-taking company was introduced in 1981, 22 licences have been granted.

Meanwhile there are 343 registered deposit-taking companies. Since April 1981, the Commissioner of Deposit-taking Companies has restricted new registrations to companies which, as well as meeting certain basic criteria such as minimum paid-up capital of $10 million, are more than 50 per cent owned by banks in Hong Kong or elsewhere. Registered deposit-taking companies are restricted to taking deposits in excess of $50,000 and of at least three months term to maturity. Neither registered nor licensed deposit-taking companies are subject to any restrictions on the rates of interest they offer.

The Commissioner of Banking, who is also the Commissioner of Deposit-taking Companies, excercises prudential supervision over all these institutions, as provided for by the Banking and Deposit-taking Companies Ordinances. Amendments made to these ordinances in 1982 empower him to obtain information on the overseas operations of Hong Kong banks and deposit-taking companies, so enabling him better to supervise their global activities and hence to play a full part in the increasingly important business of international banking supervision.

Foreign Exchange Market

Hong Kong abandoned the silver standard of its currency in 1935, when the exchange value of the Hong Kong dollar was fixed at about 1s. 3d sterling (or $15 to £1). With the setting-up of the International Monetary Fund after World War II, the Hong Kong dollar was given a gold parity reflecting this pre-war rate. The relationship between the Hong Kong dollar and sterling was, however, at no time a statutory one but was established and maintained by the operations of the Exchange Fund in conjunction with the note-issuing banks. The relationship weakened after the devaluation of the pound in November 1967, and ended after the pound was allowed to float in June 1972. The following month, the government announced the pegging of the Hong Kong dollar to the United States dollar, with provision for fluctuations of up to 2¼ per cent either side of the central rate. But in November 1974, this link was broken as well. Since that time, the Hong Kong dollar has floated independently according to market conditions (see Appendix 2).

There is now a well developed foreign exchange market where the Hong Kong dollar and other currencies are traded, mostly against the US dollar. A number of factors contribute to the market's activity: there are no exchange controls; international banks may trade through their Hong Kong offices while other centres are closed: some banks or deposit-taking companies seek to buy foreign currency as a means of holding their obligatory liquidity, while others, without a sufficient local deposit base, seek to buy Hong Kong dollars in order to fund local lending. Some of these are features peculiar to Hong Kong. Meanwhile, as in other centres, the day-to-day requirements of industry and commerce themselves ensure a considerable turnover in both the foreign exchange and other financial markets.

With effect from February 25, 1982, the government exempted interest paid on foreign currency deposits in Hong Kong from interest withholding tax, which had previously been levied at 15 per cent. (At the same time, the rate of interest tax on Hong Kong dollar deposits was reduced to 10 per cent.) The remainder of the year witnessed a very substantial expansion of foreign currency deposits held with banks and deposit-taking companies, as deposits were switched to Hong Kong from other centres and as some existing Hong Kong dollar deposits were switched into foreign currencies. All in all, the foreign currency deposit base of the monetary sector has been strengthened and the position of Hong Kong as an international financial centre enhanced.

Through its bankers the government is active in the foreign exchange market to the extent that the portfolio management considerations of the Exchange Fund require, and the timing of transactions can be varied with a view to their impact on the exchange rate of the Hong Kong dollar. The government may on occasions intervene more positively, but such intervention generally seeks only to smooth out erratic movements in the rate rather than to challenge more fundamental underlying trends.

The exchange value of the Hong Kong dollar strengthened in the early part of the year and remained quite firm well into the third quarter, no doubt helped by the narrowing of the visible trade gap. The currency was then hit by the anxieties about Hong Kong's future. Over the year as a whole the trade-weighted exchange rate index, which is calculated against the currencies of Hong Kong's 15 principal trading partners on a trade-weighted basis, showed a depreciation of 6.8 per cent. Meanwhile, reflecting in addition the marked overall strength of the United States currency, the Hong Kong dollar depreciated by 12.7 per cent against the US dollar.

Domestic Money Market

In Hong Kong wholesale transactions in the local currency are concentrated in the inter-bank market, which comprises large deposits taken by one bank or deposit-taking company from another. In particular, institutions with a local deposit base lend to those without such a base.

Other short-term instruments are less in evidence than in some other centres. There is no marketable direct government debt. Some bills of exchange are held in portfolios, but they are rarely traded. To some extent the same is true of locally issued certificates of deposit, but both the volume of such certificates in issue, and the extent to which they are traded on the secondary market, have increased considerably in the past year or so. During 1982, in the context of a long-standing commitment by the government to seek a resolution to problems which might be inhibiting the development of the secondary market for local certificates of deposit, officials held discussions with the institutions concerned. These were aimed in particular at determining whether such paper, held by banks and deposit-taking companies, could justifiably be allowed to count as a liquid asset for the purposes of meeting their statutory liquidity ratios.

The only direct government debt now outstanding is due to the Asian Development Bank, and amounted to the equivalent of $285 million at March 31, 1982. There is a small amount of marketable government-guaranteed debt, issued by government-owned bodies: this comprises $400 million of 10-year bonds and $205.75 million of five-year notes issued by the Mass Transit Railway Corporation, and $230 million of notes issued by the Hong Kong Building and Loan Agency Limited. The Mass Transit Railway Corporation also has a commercial paper facility, which was developed in 1979. The paper takes the form of negotiable bills of exchange accepted by the corporation.

Monetary Aggregates and Interest Rates

The Monetary Statistics Ordinance of 1980 paved the way for the collection of improved statistics for monitoring monetary developments. During 1982, the Hong Kong dollar money supply grew more slowly than in 1981, but the total money supply grew much more rapidly, being influenced in particular by the increase in foreign currency deposits once interest on them became exempt from interest tax.

Hong Kong dollar interest rates declined on balance during the year, largely in sympathy with similar movements in the world's major economies, particularly the United States. The government is able to exert some influence on local rates: under an operational arrangement with one of its bankers it can draw funds from, or inject funds into, the local money market thereby tightening or easing market rates. The government can have a further, limited influence in the money market by altering the mix of the Exchange Fund's deposits with banks, between those at maturities of seven days or less, against which the banks must hold 100 per cent liquidy, and those at more than seven days, against which the liquidity requirement is only 25 per cent. Meanwhile, the Hong Kong Association of Banks is obliged to consult the government regarding the level of maximum rates set under the association's interest rate rules, although any decision rests ultimately with the association.

Stock Market

The Stock Exchange of Hong Kong Limited, the company recognised for the purpose of promoting, and in due course operating, a single unified exchange in Hong Kong, celebrated the second anniversary of its incorporation in July. At the end of 1982 the company had 942 members and three associate members.

In February, a site adjacent to the Connaught Centre in Central District was sold by the government by public tender for a record price of $4,755 million. Conditions of sale of this site required the successful tenderer to provide accommodation for the unified exchange on the podium level of the building to be constructed. Construction of a twin-tower building to be called Exchange Square has commenced.

In the meantime, trading continues on the existing four exchanges. The turnover for 1982 was: Far East Exchange, $21,109 million; Hong Kong Stock Exchange, $9,858 million; Kam Ngan Stock Exchange, $15,193 million; and Kowloon Stock Exchange, $69 million. The total fo $46,229 million was 56.4 percent lower than in 1981. The Hang Seng index, having lost ground sharply after worries about Hong Kong's future came to the fore in late September and as the weakness of the property market baceme apparent, ended the year at 783.82 (July 31, 1964 = 100), compared to 1,405.82 at the end of 1981.

Staff of the office of the Commissioner for Securities continued to monitor securities transactions and to scrutinise unusual movements in the prices of securities. The year also saw the publication of the Insider Dealing Tribunal's first report. In July 1980, the tribunal had started formal hearings of an inquiry into possible insider dealing in the shares of Hutchison Whampoa

Limited at some time prior to September 26, 1979. The tribunal reported in March 1982 that there has been no insider dealing in these shares in the Hong Kong market and that it had found no evidence of culpable insider dealing elsewhere.

The Takeovers Committee, a sub-committee of the Securities Commission which is chaired by the Commissioner for Securities, continued to administer the Hong Kong Code on Takeovers and Mergers. In 1982, 14 takeovers and mergers occurred where the offeror came to hold 35 per cent or more of the voting shares of the offeree. There were also six instances of the acquisition of substantial minority stakes where shareholdings of less than 35 per cent of the voting shares were acquited. There were two instances of companies 'going public', nine rights issues and four 'shell' companies were re-activated.

During 1982, the office of the Commissioner for Securities, acting as the executive arm of the Committee on Unit Trusts, a sub-committee of the Securities Commission, continued to administer the Hong Kong Code on Unit Trusts and Mutual Funds. The number of unit trusts and mutual funds which received authorisation under the Securities Ordinance, on the recommendation of the Committee on Unit Trusts, was 15. During the year, one unit trust had its authorisation withdrawn. The total number of authorised unit trusts and mutual funds at December 31, 1982, was 87.

The combined Stock Exchanges Compensation Fund, established to compensate those who suffer pecuniary loss as a result of defaults by stockbrokers, amounted to $25 million on December 31, 1982. Deposits lodged by dealers other than stockbrokers stood at $12 million. The purpose of these deposits is to give some protection to investors against any defaults by dealers who are not members of a stock exchange.

At the end of 1982, 2,931 individuals and corporations were registered under the Securities (Dealers, Investments Advisers and Representatives) Regulations 1974.

Commodity Exchange and Gold Markets

The Hong Kong Commodity Exchange Limited is the one company licensed under the Commodities Trading Ordinance to operate a commodity exchange trading in futures contracts in Hong Kong. It operates four futures markets: cotton, sugar, soybeans and gold. The turnovers reported on these four markets for 1982 were: cotton, no trading; sugar, 350,977 lots of 50 long tons each; soybeans, 747,943 lots of 30,000 kg each; gold, 10,910 lots of 100 troy ounces each.

In June 1982, the Commodities Trading Ordinance was amended so as to increase substantially the penalties for dealing by unregistered dealers. The ordinance now provides for a maximum penalty of $500,000 and five years' imprisonment for carrying on a business of dealing in commodity futures contracts while unregistered.

A working party was established during the year, under the chairmanship of the Commissioner for Commodities Trading, to review the operation of the Hong Kong Commodity Exchange and to consider whether the terms of the exchange's licence require modification. A major review of the Commodities Trading Ordinance has also been put in hand. The Hong Kong Commodity Exchange has set up a working party to study the possible establishment of a financial futures market.

At the end of 1982, 1,483 individuals, corporations and firms were registered under the Commodities Trading (Dealers, Commodity Trading Advisers and Representatives) Regulations 1976.

The Commodity Exchange Compensation Fund, established to compensate those who suffer pecuniary loss as a result of default by shareholders of the exchange, amounted to $8 million at the end of the year. Deposits lodged by dealers, other than shareholders of the Hong Kong Commodity Exchange, stood at $1 million. The purpose of these deposits is to give some protection to investors against any defaults by dealers who are not shareholders of the exchange.

Trading in gold on the Chinese Gold and Silver Exchange Society was fairly active in 1982, while membership of the society remained closed at 194 member firms. Prices, after allowing for exchange rate fluctuations, paralleled those in the other major markets of London, Zurich and New York, rising from $2,714 per tael of 99 per cent fine gold at the end of 1981 to $3,492 at the end of 1982. (One tael is equal to 37.429 grams.)

The international gold market in Hong Kong continued to grow during the year. Dealings principally take place in US dollars per troy ounce of 99.95 per cent fine gold, with delivery in London. The price of gold loco London rose from US$400 per troy ounce at the end of 1981 to US$448 at the end of 1982.

Appendix 2

Exchange Value of the Hong Kong Dollar (continued)

(A) When a fixed exchange rate was maintained against one or more other currencies

	Par value of the HK$ in grams of fine gold	£1 = HK$	US$1 = HK$	SDR1 = HK$
December 18, 1946 IMF parities established: Hong Kong dollar is pegged to sterling	0.223834	16.00	3.970	
September 18, 1949 Hong Kong dollar devalued *pari passu* with sterling by 30.5%	0.155517	16.00	5.714	
November 20, 1967 Hong Kong dollar devalued *pari passu* with sterling by 14.3%	0.133300	16.00	6.667	
November 23, 1967 Hong Kong dollar revalued by 10%, including against sterling, but continues pegged to sterling, at new rate	0.146631	14.55	6.061	
December 18, 1971 As part of the general currency realignment, Hong Kong dollar and sterling appreciate by 8.57% against US dollar. As a result of USA terminating, in August 1971, the convertibility of US dollar into gold, gold par value no longer has a practical meaning. IMF begins to adopt the SDR as its accounting unit		14.55	5.582	6.061

July 6, 1972

Hong Kong dollar pegged to US dollar following the floating of sterling   5.650   6.134

February 14, 1973

US dollar devalued; Hong Kong dollar remains pegged at new rate   5.085   6.134

November 26, 1974

Hong Kong dollar allowed to float, ie the government no longer undertakes to maintain a particular rate against any other currency

(B) Since the currency was floated

End of period	£	US$	DM	¥	SDR	Trade-weighted Index* (18.12.71 = 100)
		(HK dollars to one unit of foreign currency)				
1974	11.53	4.910	2.03	0.0164	6.012	105.9
1980	12.27	5.130	2.61	0.0253	6.543	88.2
1981	10.88	5.675	2.52	0.0260	6.605	85.9
1982	10.58	6.495	2.73	0.0278	7.165	80.1

Note: * The trade-weighted exchange rate index is derived from a weighted average of nominal exchange rates of the Hong Kong dollar against the currencies of 15 principal trading partners.

Source: *Hong Kong Annual Report 1983*, (Hong Kong: Government Printer, 1983).

Appendix 3

International Commercial Relations[1]

Hong Kong's external commercial relations are conducted by the Trade Department within the framework of a basically free trade policy. Hong Kong practises, to the full, the rules of the General Agreement on Tariffs and Trade (GATT). Virtually the only restrictions maintained on trade are those required by international obligations. Most prominent among these are restraints on textile exports to major trading partners in Europe and North America. All these restraint arrangements were negotiated under the Arrangement Regarding International Trade in Textiles, commonly known as the Multi-Fibre Arrangement (MFA). A feature of the MFA is the Textiles Surveillance Body (TSB) which supervises its implementation. A Hong Kong representative sat on the TSB as an alternate member to the representative of the Republic of Korea in 1982.

The third term of the MFA, for four years and seven months, came into effect on January 1, 1982. It has been accepted by Hong Kong and over 40 countries, including Hong Kong's major trading partners.

Co-ordination among developing exporting members of the MFA which contributed significantly to the preservation of their interests during its renegotiation in 1981, continued in 1982. At the two formal co-ordination meetings held in Geneva in April and August/September, developing exporting members arrived at a common interpretation of certain provisions of the protocol extending the MFA and exchanged views on their bilateral textile negotiations with developed importing countries. Hong Kong participated in both meetings.

Following two rounds of textile negotiations held in Feburary and March, a bilateral agreement was concluded covering Hong Kong's exports of cotton, man-made fibre and wool textiles to the United States. The agreement has a duration of six years from January 1, 1982, and incorporates a new restraint structure. Exports in 24 categories of textile products are subject to specific restraint while exports in all other categories, constituting one-third of Hong Kong's textile exports to the United States, have been liberalised. These latter

1. Hong Kong Annual Report, (Hong Kong: Government Printer, 1983).

categories have been placed under an export authorisation surveillance system operated by the Trade Department.

The bilateral textiles agreement between Hong Kong and the European Economic Community covering the five years commencing 1978 expired at the end of 1982. Following negotiations under the MFA, a new bilateral agreement was concluded with the EEC which has a duration of four years from January 1983, and covers all Hong Kong's exports of cotton, man-made fibres and wool textiles, to the EEC. Under the new agreement, exports in 46 categories of textile products are subject to quantitative restraint, while exports in the remaining categories are subject to the department's Export Authorisation System.

Negotiations between Hong Kong and Canada were held in February 1982 with a view to concluding a long-term agreement governing most of Hong Kong's exports of cotton, man-made fibre and wool textiles to Canada. As a result of these negotiations, an agreement of five years' duration was reached with effect from January 1, 1982. The agreement provides for specific restraint on 16 textile categories while exports in 10 other categories are subject to the export authorisation surveillance system.

Under the MFA, bilateral agreements were renegotiated during the year with Finland, Switzerland and Austria. The agreement concluded with Sweden in 1981 remains effective until March 1983. Under the terms of the agreements, exports of certain textiles from Hong Kong to these countries were placed under restraint or surveillance.

Norway's action against certain textile imports, which was introduced on January 1, 1979, under Article XIX of the GATT, remained in force during the year. The action was in the form of global import quotas, but it had a discriminatory effect against Hong Kong. Following a complaint made by Hong Kong to the GATT Council in July 1979, a GATT panel, in its report submitted to the GATT Council in March 1980, concluded that Norway had failed to make its action consistent with Article XIII of the GATT by not allocating to Hong Kong an appropriate share of the so-called global quotas; such a measure constituting *prima-facie* a case of nullification or impairment of Hong Kong's rights under the GATT. Notwithstnading the GATT Council's adoption in principle of the report in June 1980 and recommendation to the Norwegian Government to make its action consistent with the GATT as soon as possible, bilateral consultations subsequently held between the two governments failed to resolve the issue.

France maintains quantitative restrictions against imports from Hong Kong in respect of a number of products, including quartz watches. Hong Kong believes that the French action is discriminatory against Hong Kong and is in contravention of France's obligations under the GATT. Several rounds of consultations on the issue were held with the Commission of the European Communities, representing France, but did not produce a mutually acceptable solution. As a result, in September 1982 Hong Kong requested the GATT to convene a panel to consider its complaints against the French action and to make a ruling on the matter.

A major event in GATT activities during 1982 was the ministerial meeting held in November in which Hong Kong participated fully. The meeting was designed to give impetus to improve the multilateral trading system. At the meeting, ministers discussed the problems affecting the trading system, the position of developing countries in the world trade, future prospects for the development of trade, and future priorities for co-operation among GATT contracting parties. The meeting concluded with the adoption of a ministerial declaration whereby the contracting parties of the GATT reaffirmed their commitment to abide by their GATT obligations and to further liberalise international trade. The declaration also covered various specific issues, of which the most significant to Hong Kong concerned world trade in textiles and clothing. It was agreed that an in-depth study on that sector of trade and an examination of the methods of procedure of further liberalisation would be carried out speedily.

Generalised schemes of preference are operated by most developed countries to promote the export of goods from developing countries and territories. Apart from Finland, all developed countries operating such schemes include Hong Kong as a beneficiary. The schemes allow duty-free or reduced tariff entry for most agricultural and industrial products from beneficiaries, but certain products from Hong Kong are specifically excluded from the schemes operated by Australia, Austria, Japan, Norway, Switzerland and the USA. Hong Kong has consistently made it clear that it seeks no special advantages under these schemes, but simply treatment similar to that accorded to close competitors. The difference in treatment has been the subject of continuing official exchanges which have resulted in gradual improvement of Hong Kong's position in certain schemes. In 1982, Switzerland decided to phase out by 1983 the unfavourable tariff treatment for two products from Hong Kong under its scheme.

Appendix 4

Hong Kong's Growing Economic Relations With China[1]

Situated on the doorstep of the world's most populous nation, Hong Kong has always played a major role as an entrepot for trade between China and the outside world.

This role has expanded and contracted in line with China's policies regarding external contact. With the advent of the open-door economic policy under the present Chinese leadership, Hong Kong's business relations with the mainland have grown dramatically in the past four years.

China is now deeply committed to raising the standard of living of its people through the implementation of the "four modernizations." This will entail a massive increase in the country's imports of capital, technology and goods as well as a steady build up in exports over the next few decades.

Hong Kong's key role as a channel for these expanding external economic relations has been acknowledged by China; hence their leaders' deep interest in maintaining the territory's present status as a free port and major international business center. Hong Kong has the capability to assist China's modernization efforts in financing, international marketing, production technology, infrastructure development and many other areas.

Likewise, Hong Kong is ideally placed to play an increasingly important role as the base from which overseas organizations can participate in China's development programs.

Before 1981, China has been Hong Kong's third largest trading partner after the U.S.A. and Japan. Total bilateral trade was valued at HK$ 17,048 million (US$ 2,622 million) in 1979, an increase of 57 percent over 1978, and HK$ 28, 195 million (US$ 4,337 million) in 1980, up by 65 percent over the preceding year. During 1981, China overtook Japan as Hong Kong's second largest trading partner, and held that position in 1982. Last year, trade grew by

(Exchange Rate Used Throughout: HK$ 6.5 + US$ 1)

1. *Hong Kong's Economy,* (Hong Kong: Trade Development Council, 1983).

11 percent and China accounted for 16.6 percent (HK$ 44,733 million, US$ 6,822 million) of Hong Kong's total trade.

Hong Kong has always incurred deficits in trading with China and in 1982 this deficit increased by 14 percent to HK$ 21,137 million (US$ 3,251 million).

In the 1978-81 period, Hong Kong's imports from China rose at an average annual growth rate of 41 percent from HK$ 10,550 million (US$ 1,623 million) to HK$ 29,510 million (US$ 4,54 million). In 1982, despite a slowdown in the growth rate (+12 percent), China overtook Japan to become Hong Kong's leading supplier, with total shipments amounting to HK$ 32,935 million (US$ 5,066 million).

Last year 24 percent of total imports from China into Hong Kong were foodstuffs. Raw materials and semi-manufactures accounted for 30 percent (mainly textile yarn and fabics, crude animal and vegetable materials, and construction materials) and consumer goods represented 35 percent (mainly clothing, textile "made-up" articles, footwear and household ware). Hong Kong's other imports from China include fuels and capital goods.

Of Hong Kong's total imports from China, about 45 percent were reexported to other countries in 1982, compared with 31 percent in 1977. Hong Kong reexports of Chinese origin goods accounted for an increasing proportion of its total imports from China in the last few years, reflecting the renewed importance of Hong Kong as a transshipment center as a result of China's modernization drive. During 1982, Hong Kong's reexports of Chinese origin increased by 31 percent to HK$ 14,694 million (US$ 2,260 million).

In 1978, Hong Kong's domestic exports to China grew by 159 percent, followed by another 643 percent rise in 1979 to HK$ 603 million (US$ 92,769 million). As a result, China became Hong Kong's 15th largest market in the world in that year. Further strong growth rates of 166 percent in 1980, 82 per cent in 1981 and 30 percent in 1982 (to HK$ 3,806 million, US$ 585 million) raised China to Hong Kong's fourth largest market.

Major exports to China include textile yarn and fabrics, telecommunications equipment and parts, watches and clocks, clothing, toys and games, plastic articles, electric current, tobacco, radio broadcast receivers and polymerization and copolymerization products. While part of the rapid growth of Hong Kong exports to China is in goods for consumption (e.g. watches and clocks, sound equipment, toys and garments), it is notable that under numerous compensation trade and processing arrangements, semi-manufactures and machinery have been exported into China and most of the final products are imported into or through Hong Kong. This process is likely to remain a significant factor in the expansion of trade between Hong Kong and China.

During 1980, Hong Kong's reexports to China rose by 253 percent to HK$ 4,642 million (US$ 714 million), and further 73 percent to HK$ 8,044 million (US$ 1,237 million) in 1981. Despite a 1 percent decline to HK$ 7,992 million

(US$ 1,299 million) in 1982, China remained the largest market for Hong Kong reexports with a 18 percent of the total.

These reexports to China were comprised of textiles (accounting for 33 percent of the total in 1982), crude vegetable materials, textile and leather machinery, artificial resins and plastic materials, telecommunications equipment and parts, watches and clocks, television receivers, motor vehicles and electronic components.

In parallel with the growth in trade, Hong Kong has participated extensively in China's industrial development in recent years. In its modernization drive, China introduced several forms of cooperation—"joint ventures," "cooperative production ventures," "compensation trade," and "processing and assembling agreements"—to attract overseas manufacturers to enter into arrangements for the production of a wide range of products, particularly in a number of designated "special economic zones" in Shenzhen, Zhuhai, Shantou and Xiamen. A large number of Hong Kong industrialists have travelled to China and increasing numbers of them have either entered into, or are in the late stages of concluding, trade arrangements of one kind or another with the Chinese authorities.

Up to June 1982, 43 equity joint ventures had been approved in China, involving total investment of over HK$ 1,300 million (US$ 200 million). Of this amount, Hong Kong investment accounted for the largest share of HK$ 260 million (US$ 40 million), covering 21 enterprises. According to the latest reported figures, total investment commitments in Shenzhen special economic zone—China's largest SEZ—amounted to HK$ 8.86 billion (US$ 1.36 billion) at the end of the third quarter 1982. Of this, the Shenzhen SEZ Development Company had signed 51 large projects which alone accounted HK$ 8 billion (US$ 1.23 billion). The remaining investment came from nearly 1,400 agreements, mostly of the compensation trade. About 90 percent of the total investment in Shenzhen is reported to be from Hong Kong.

Looking to the future, Hong Kong—as China's commercial gateway to the outside world—is likely to play a greatly expanded role in all aspects of the "four modernizations."

While it is true that China can turn to many different countries for assistance in its development, geographical proximity and a common language and culture make Hong Kong a uniquely convenient source.

More importantly, it can be argued that the recent and directly relevant experience that many Hong Kong businessmen have in industrialization is more appropriate to China's current state of development than the most advanced technology from Europe, North America and Japan—all of which experienced their own industrial revolutions too long ago to have much practical relevance to China.

Hong Kong's contribution to China's modernization permeates every area of the economy. Already the largest source of hard currency earnings, Hong

Kong should continue to play an important and growing role in China's efforts to generate the foreign exchange resources it needs to build up its industrial base. Hong Kong not only takes about a quarter of China's visible exports, but is also a major source of remittances from overseas Chinese, returns on capital investments by China in the territory and tourist spending.

It has been estimated that, of China's total foreign exchange earnings, some 35 percent are generated in or through Hong Kong; in value terms approximately HK$ 40 billion (US$ 6 billion) annually.

The converse side of Hong Kong's extensive investments in China is the territory's value in terms of China's own investments. China is thought to have invested about HK$ 20-30 billion (US$ 3-5 billion) in Hong Kong; largely in business ventures like banking, insurance, shipping, retailing, property and manufacturing. With its combination of a western style economy, free and open market and Chinese culture, Hong Kong serves as a uniquely convenient "laboratory" for China's growing commercial operations; a place where they can secure all the experience that the free capitalist world provides. In particular, Hong Kong offers a reservoir of skill and technical expertise which China wishes to tap and study.

Being one of the world's leading financial and banking centers, Hong Kong offers a wide range of banking and financial facilities which greatly assist investors in China, and its deep sea port serves southern China's import and export requirements.

In addition, there is Hong Kong's position as the primary entry point for tourists and our emerging role as a support base for certain aspects of China's oil development.

Most commentators now agree that the pragmatic Chinese leaders are not likely to compromise their own economic programs by taking any action which might adversely affect Hong Kong's business climate and businessmen in the territory are confidently looking forward to a bright and busy future.

Appendix 5

Industrial Investment[1]

Hong Kong Government practises a noninterventionist policy and neither favors nor discriminates against investment by foreign- or locally-based companies. In terms of attracting foreign investments, Hong Kong is one of the prime targets in the Asia/Pacific region though it offers no tax holidays, special subsidies nor other inducements often found in developing countries. Instead, Hong Kong's main attractions are its centralized location in the region; its stable government which offers consistent policies and is a staunch upholder of the free market principles and its lack of bureaucratic red tape, foreign exchange controls and other restrictions on capital or profit repatriation or local equity holding requirements.

The accumulated total of foreign investment capital recorded up to the end of 1982 in Hong Kong's manufacturing industries amounted to HK$ 9,500 million of which HK$ 7,560 million came directly from overseas sources with the remainder contributed by local interests in the form of joint venture. Investment in the territory sector is much higher and many foreign-based corporations, banks, traders, airline and shipping agencies, etc. make Hong Kong their regional headquarters and main springboard to the markets of Asia, especially China.

The leading foreign investors in Hong Kong are the Americans with HK$ 3,526 million or 47 percent of total foreign investment in Hong Kong's manufacturing industries as recorded up to the end of 1982; Japan with HK$ 2,278 million or 30 percent; United Kingdom with HK$ 448 million or 6 percent; Switzerland with HK$ 200 million and the Netherlands with HK$ 189 million. Other investors included Denmark, Australia, Taiwan, Singapore, France, Philippines, West Germany, and Thailand. The major industry targets of these investments are electronics, textiles and clothing, building and construction materials, chemical products, food and beverage, watches and clocks, and accessories. These investments are spread over 438 establishments employing 92,803 people. Of this amount, 299 were wholly owned overseas interests while the rest were joint ventures between overseas and Hong Kong interests.

1. Major portion of this appendix adopted from *Hong Kong's Economy,* (Hong Kong: Trade Development Council, 1983).

Appendix 6

The Questionnaire

QUESTIONNAIRE FOR A SURVEY OF CHANNEL
STRATEGY FOR EXPORT DISTRUBUTION
出口經路戰累研究問卷

1. When was your company established?   Year _____

2. What is the ownership status of your company?
   Public (with shareholders) _____   Private (sole ownership / partnership) _____

3. Which of the following manufacturing industries does your company belong?
   Clothing _____   Electronics_____

4. Please give the total export sales of your company in the years stated below:
   (Rounded estimation will suffice)
   1980 _____   1979 _____   1978 _____   1977 _____

5. How many employees does your company have now? (Check one)
   _____ Below 50   _____ 50-99   _____ 100-149
   _____ 150-199   _____ 200-250   _____ Above 250

6. How long has your company been in the export business? (Check one)
   _____ Less than 2 yrs   _____ 2-4 yrs   _____ 5-7 yrs
   _____ 8-10 yrs   _____ Over 10 yrs

7. Please estimate the percentage of your exports going to the following areas:

Export Market	in 1979	in 1980
North America	_____ %	_____ %
Western Europe	_____ %	_____ %
South & Central America	_____ %	_____ %
Asia & Pacific	_____ %	_____ %
Africa & Middle East	_____ %	_____ %
Others	_____ %	_____ %

8. Looking at your industry (Clothing or Electronic) as a whole, how would you
   evaluate its performance in recent years? (Check one)

   Very Successful ____ Quite Successful ____ Average ____ Quite Unsuccessful ____ Very Unsuccessful ____

9. How would you rate your company's export performance in the past few years
   relative to the "average" firm in the industry? (Check one)

   Highly Above Average ____ Above Average ____ Average ____ Below Average ____ Highly Below Average ____

10. Over the past four years, what changes have taken place in your company's goals
    regarding export program?

    The company's goals regarding export program have: (Check one)
    _____ Become more committed towards expansion
    _____ Remained practically the same
    _____ Moved towards reduction

11. Suppose that your company decided to expand your export program, how important would each of the following marketing variables be? (Check the appropriate space on each scale)

	Highly Important	Important	Slightly Important
Product 慮高) (eg. Product Improvement)	_____	_____	_____
Distribution Channel(經路) (eg. Refinement)	_____	_____	_____
Price(價格) (eg. Price discount)	_____	_____	_____
Promotion(推廣) (eg. More allocation)	_____	_____	_____

12. Please rank the following international environmental factors which hinder your exports by distributing 100 points among them (more points indicate greater hindrance).

Cultural Differences _____
Quotas and Tariffs _____
Foreign Competition _____
Market Demand _____
Transportation Costs _____
Others (Please specify) _____

_____

100
=========

13. With the increase in overseas competition and trade restrictions in importing countries, has the proportion of export channel functions(出口經路職能) (such as financing inventory, financing and developing promotional programs, and other service or financial functions) performed by your company increased, decreased, or remained the same? (Check one)

Increased Substantially	Increased Moderately	Remained the Same	Decreased Moderately	Decreased Substantially

14. What was the title of the executive in charge of your company's export activity during initial commencement of export operations? _____

To whom did he report (Title): _____

How much time did he spent on export matters? Full-time _____ *Part-time _____
*If answer is Part-time, please give the percentage of time spent on export matters: _____ %

15. How were your company's export channel functions handled during the initial years of export operations?

During the initial years of export operations, the company's export channel functions were handled by: (Check as appropriate)
_____ Hong Kong Based Resident Buyer (eg. Buying office of foreign firm)
_____ Hong Kong Based Export Buying Agent (eg. Broker in Hong Kong)
_____ Hong Kong Based Export Merchant (eg. Trading company in Hong Kong)
_____ Hong Kong Based Export Agent (eg. Import & export firm in Hong Kong)
_____ Export Department within your Company
_____ Foreign Based Agent (eg. Foreign broker)
_____ Foreign Based Merchant (eg. Foreign wholesaler)
_____ Foreign Sales Office or Branch of your Company
_____ Others (Please specify) _____

How many of the above alternative channels were considered? 1 2 3 4 5 Over

What were the criteria for selecting channel(篩選準據)? (Check as appropriate)

_____ Market Potential   _____ Market Area Served   _____ Growth Plan
_____ Experience   _____ Financial Strength   _____ Others

16. What is the title of the executive in charge of your company's export activity NOW? _____

    To whom does he report (Title): _____

    How much time does he spend on export matters?   Full-time _____   **Part-time _____
    **If answer is Part-time, please give the percentage of time spend on
        export matters: _____ %

17. How are your company's export channel functions handled NOW?

    Today, the company's export channel functions are handled by: (Check as
                                                                    appropriate)
    _____ Hong Kong Based Resident Buyer (eg. Buying office of foreign firm)
    _____ Hong Kong Based Export Buying Agent (eg. Broker in Hong Kong)
    _____ Hong Kong Based Export Merchant (eg. Trading company in Hong Kong)
    _____ Hong Kong Based Export Agent (eg. Import & export firm in Hong Kong)
    _____ Export Department within your Company
    _____ Foreign Based agent (eg. Foreign Broker)
    _____ Foreign Based Merchant (eg. Foreign wholesaler)
    _____ Foreign Sales Office or Branch of your Company
    _____ Others (Please specify) _____

    How many of the above alternative channels were considered? 1 2 3 4 5 Over

    What were the criteria for selecting channel? (Check as appropriate)

    _____ Market Potential   _____ Market Area Served   _____ Growth Plan
    _____ Experience   _____ Financial Strength   _____ Others

18. Does your company have its own sales offices or branches in foreign markets?

    *Yes _____   **No _____

    *If YES, which of the following market areas: (Check as appropriate)

                    _____ North America   _____ Africa & Middle East
                    _____ Western Europe   _____ South & Central America
                    _____ Asia & Pacific   _____ Others

    **If NO, will your company be planning on setting up sales offices or
        branches in foreign markets during the next five years?

        _____   _____   _____   _____   _____
         Very   Likely   Undecided   Unlikely   Very
        Likely   Unlikely

19. If your company has relied on outside channel agencies or institutions to
    perform a portion or all of your channel functions(經銷機能), are you
    satisfied with the performance of these channel agencies or institutions?
    (Check the appropriate space on each scale)

	Highly Satisfied	Satisfied	Dissatisfied	Highly Dissatisfied
Cooperativeness				
Dependability				
Intelligence				
Competence				
Others (Please specify)				

20. Who are the executives involved in evaluating the performance of the export
    distribution channel(評估出口經銷結訊)? (Check as appropriate)

    _____ Top Management   _____ Accounting   _____ Marketing
    _____ Production   _____ Finance   _____ Sales
    _____ Others (Please specify) _____

    How often is the evaluation performed? (Check one)

    _____ Monthly   _____ Quarterly   _____ Semi-annually
    _____ Annually   _____ Others (Please specify) _____

How much time is spent each year evaluating the export distribution channel?
(Check one)

:_____:_____:_____:_____:_____:_____:
Extremely   Substantially
Nominal Amount   Large Amount

What evaluative criteria are used?   (Check as appropriate)

_____ Market Share	_____ Gross Margin	_____ Investment
_____ Cost	_____ Sales	_____ Service
_____ Others		

21. Based on your experience, which events have led to a modification of the export
distribution channel?   (Check as appropriate)

_____ Changes in Demand	_____ Product Changes
_____ Competition	_____ New Markets
_____ Changes in Sales	_____ Changes in Profitability
_____ Customer Needs	_____ Loss of Market Share
_____ Changes in Cost	_____ Others (Please specify)
	_____

THANK YOU FOR YOUR PARTICIPATION IN THIS SURVEY

Appendix 7

Cover Letter to the Questionnaire

C.U.G.P. 6 5000-10-77

THE CHINESE UNIVERSITY OF HONG KONG　香港中文大學

SHATIN · NT · HONG KONG · TEL. 12-612211 · CABLE ADDRESS · SINOVERSITY ·　香港新界沙田 · 電話：一二 · 六一二二壹一

Department of Marketing and International Business　　　　　　　　工 商 管 理 學 院
Faculty of Business Administration　　　　　　　　　　　　　　　　市 場 與 國 際 企 業 學 系

Ref.

<u>CONFIDENTIAL</u>

QUESTIONNAIRE FOR THE RESEARCH PROJECT
ON CHANNEL STRATEGY FOR EXPORT DISTRIBUTION
出 口 經 路 戰 累 研 究 問 卷

Dear Sir/Madame,

The purpose of this questionnaire is to survey executives in
selected industries regarding export distribution. This survey is
an important part of the study which explores channel strategy for
export distribution of Hong Kong manufacturing firms. The findings
of this study and the methodological framework to be developed can
have important implications for managers in Hong Kong.

In order to complete the empirical section of this study,
you are kindly requested to complete all questions in the questionnaire (except where otherwise stated).

I assure you that all the questionnaire materials will be
treated as strictly confidential. Under no circumstances will the
identity of the respondent or that of his/her company be revealed.

It will be much appreciated if you can complete the questionnaire at your earliest convenience and return it in the enclosed
self-addressed envelope.

Thank you very much for your participation.

Yours sincerely,

T. S. Chan
Lecturer and Project
Coordinator

Encl.

Appendix 8

The Interview Guide

INTERVIEW GUIDE

Name of Company:

Address:

Telephone:

Industry Code: 1 = Clothing   2 = Electronics

Name and position of Interviewee:

Date of Completion:

---

1. General Background

    --Company goals and objectives
    --Marketing objectives
    --Channel objectives
    --Company policy affecting distribution channel

2. How do you see as the role of Distribution Channel in the coming five years?

3. What events would lead to changes in your company's channel functions for export distribution?

4. What structural or operational changes have taken place since the initiation of export operations in your company?

5. How do you feel about direct versus indirect exporting?

6. Have your company made any previous attempt to seek greater control over the distribution of exports? Why or Why not? How?

7. As the volume of exports increases, will your answer to Question 6 change in any other way?

8. a. Who are your major competitors (domestic and foreign)? How do your competitors distribute their products?

    b. With the threat of increased foreign competition, will your channel strategy be affected?

9. a. To what extent does the imposition of quotas and tariffs by the United States and Western Europe affect your company's export sales?

    b. What impact does your answer to Question 9a have on your channel strategy?

10. What role does channel planning play in the attainment of your company's export objectives? How systematic is your company's strategic marketing planning?

Appendix 9

Current Modifications in Hong Kong's Quota Allocation System

Hong Kong first agreed to restrict its exports of textiles in 1959. At present, Hong Kong has bilateral agreements under the MultiFiber Arrangement with Austria, Canada, and E.E.C., Finland, Sweden, Switzerland and the United States. The Trade, Industry and Custom Department of the Hong Kong government is responsible for allocating quotas to local manufacturers within the terms of bilateral agreements.

Under the first modification of the quota system in 1976, the Trade Industry and Custom Department divided up the total number of quotas annually among companies on the basis of past export performance. If more than half of the quotas allocated to a firm has been used, then the same share of quotas will be renewed for the next year. In addition, if the usage rate is over 95 percent, then there is an additional growth bonus. The government also has a small pool of quotas for new firms on a first-come, first-served basis.

A firm can temporarily transfer unused proportions of their quota allocations. However, there is a penalty of a reduction in quotas by an amount equal to 50 percent of the transfer, if the firm transfers 50 percent of its allocation during two successive years. This leads to "quota farming," whereby one garment manufacturer would sell the right to export a certain number of garment to another garment manufacturer for a price. It is often claimed by local manufacturers that some quota holders make money simply from sales of their quotas rather than from manufacturing.

In July 1980, a modified system was introduced. The 50 percent cutoff level has been abolished, so that a company which has used 49 percent of its 100,000 dozen of a particular clothing item will not be penalized while another company which has used 50 percent of its 10,000 dozen of the same clothing item is entitled to renewal of allocation. The bonus quota will be allocated only to company which utilized 95 percent or more of its allocation through its own manufacturing. New manufacturer that qualifies as a "persistent transferee"— buyer of quotas amounting to more than 50 percent of its own allocation for two years—will be eligible for an increase in its quota allocation.

To prevent habitual transfer (instead of manufacturing), the penalty rules are expanded. Maximum allowable transfer will be calculated on a per-market and per-product group basis instead of the old calculation which based on the entire quota holdings in each market.

Notes

Chapter 1

1. *Hong Kong Annual Report 1983*, (Hong Kong: Government Printer, 1983).

2. *Hong Kong Monthly Digest of Statistics,* various issues, (Hong Kong: Government Printer, 1983).

3. Ibid.

Chapter 2

1. *Hong Kong Statistics,* various years, (Hong Kong: Government Printer, 1950-60).

2. E.F. Szczepanik, *The Economic Growth of Hong Kong,* (London: Oxford Press, 1960), p. 141.

3. *Hong Kong Monthly Digest of Statistics,* (Hong Kong: Census and Statistics Department, January 1983).

4. *Hong Kong Annual Report 1983,* (Hong Kong: Government Printer, 1983).

5. Ibid.

6. Ibid.

7. John Boyer, "The Widening of Hong Kong's Economic Base," *Proceedings of the Conference on Diversification of Hong Kong Industry,* (Hong Kong: Hong Kong Management Association, 1978).

8. *Hong Kong Annual Report 1983,* (Hong Kong: Government Printer, 1983).

9. Ibid.

10. *Hong Kong into the 80's: Industrial Investment,* (Hong Kong: Government Printer, 1981).

11. Cheng, T.Y., *The Economy of Hong Kong,* (Hong Kong: Far East Publications, 1978).

12. *Hong Kong Monthly Digest of Statistics,* various issues, (Hong Kong: Government Printer, 1977-83), and *Hong Kong's Economy,* (Hong Kong: Trade Development Council, 1983). Most of the statistics in this section were obtained from these sources.

13. *Hong Kong's Economy,* (Hong Kong: Trade Development Council, 1983).

14. Ibid.

15. Ibid.

16.   *Hong Kong Review of Overseas Trade in 1979,* (Hong Kong: Census and Statistics Department, 1980).

17.   "Foreign Economic Trends: Hong Kong," (Hong Kong: American Consulate General, February 1979).

18.   Yao, Y.C., *Banking and Currency in Hong Kong,* (London: Macmillan, 1974), p. 143.

19.   *Hang Seng Economic Quarterly,* (Hong Kong: Hang Seng Bank, April 1983).

Chapter 3

1.   Claire Selltiz, Marie Jahoda, Morton Deutsch, and Stuart Cook, *Research Methods in Social Relations,* (New York: Holt, Rinehart and Winston, Inc., 1962), p. 50.

2.   Ibid.

3.   *Members' Directory of the Federation of Hong Kong Industries,* (Hong Kong: Federation of Hong Kong Industries, 1978).

4.   Although both Chinese and English are official languages in Hong Kong, Chinese is much preferred among Chinese businessmen.

5.   The Hong Kong Management Association is a government-sponsored organization for the advancement of management in Hong Kong.

Chapter 4

1.   Nie, Norman H., C.H. Hull, J.G. Jenkins, K. Steinbrenner and D. Bent. *Statistical Packages for the Social Sciences,* Second Edition, (New York: McGraw Hill, 1975).

2.   A detailed description of Hong Kong's involvement in M.F.A. can be found in Appendix III.

3.   *Hong Kong Annual Report 1983,* (Hong Kong: Government Printer, 1983).

4.   Most of the statistics in this section were from *Hong Kong's Economy,* (Hong Kong: Trade Development Council, 1983).

5.   *Hong Kong Annual Report 1983,* (Hong Kong: Government Printer, 1983).

6.   Ibid.

7.   Statistics in this section from *Hong Kong's Economy,* (Hong Kong: Trade Development Council, 1983).

8.   *Hong Kong Monthly Digest of Statistics,* (Hong Kong: Government Printer, January 1983).

9.   Percentages are rounded off to the nearest percentage point.

10.   Further cross-tabulation by industry is not possible because of the small number of respondents (14 firms) from the electronics industry.

Chapter 5

1.   The Hong Kong Trade Development Council is a government statutory body established in 1966. Its main responsibility is to promote and develop international trade with special emphasis on Hong Kong's exports.

2.   This portion of the chapter is substantially adapted from a paper being developed by T.S. Chan and J.C. Miller.

Bibliography

Books

Abdel-Malek, Talaat, *Managerial Export-Orientation: A Canadian Study,* School of Business Administration, University of Western Ontario, London, Canada, 1974.

Alderson, Wroe, "Factors Governing the Development of Marketing Channels," in R.M. Clewett (ed.), *Marketing Channels for Manufactured Products,* Richard D. Irwin, Homewood, Ill., 1954.

Balderston, F.E., "Design of Marketing Channels," *Theory in Marketing,* Reavis Cox, Wroe Alderson, and Stanley J. Shapiro, eds., Richard D. Irwin, Homewood, Ill., 1964.

Baligh, Hemley H., "A Theoretical Framework for Channel Choice," in P.D. Bennett, *Economic Growth, Competition and World Markets,* American Marketing Association, Chicago, 1965.

Beazer, William F., *The Commercial Future of Hong Kong,* Praeger Studies, New York, 1978.

Bickers, R.L.T., *Export Marketing in Europe,* Gower Press, London, 1971.

Bowersox, Donald J., M. Bixby Cooper, Douglas M. Lambert, and Donald A. Taylor, *Management in Marketing Channels,* McGraw Hill, New York, 1980.

Breyer, Ralph F., "Some Observations on Structural Formation and the Growth of Marketing Channels," *Theory in Marketing,* Reavis Cox, Wroe Alderson, and Stanley J. Shapiro, eds., Richard D. Irwin, Homewood Ill., 1964.

Bucklin, Louis P., *A Theory of Distribution Structure,* Institute of Business and Economic Research, University of California, Berkeley, 1966.

Cheng, T.Y., *The Economy of Hong Kong,* Far East Publications, Hong Kong, 1978.

Farmer, Richard N. and Barry M. Richaman, *International Business,* 3rd Edition, Cedarwood Press, Bloomington, Ind., 1980.

Hirsch, Seev, *The Export Performance of Six Manufacturing Industries,* Praeger Publishers, New York, 1971.

Johnson, James C. and Donald F. Wood, *Contemporary Physical Distribution,* Petroleum Publishing Co., 1977.

Kahler, Ruel and Roland L. Kramer, *International Marketing,* South Western Publishing Co., Chicago Ill., 1977.

Keegan, Warren, *Multinational Marketing Management,* Prentice-Hall Inc., Englewood Cliffs, New Jersey, 1974.

Kollat, David T., Roger Blackwell and James F. Robeson, *Strategic Marketing,* Holt, Rinehart and Winston, Inc., New York, 1972.

Kotler, Philip, *Marketing Management: Analysis, Planning and Control,* 2nd Edition, Prentice-Hall Inc., Englewood Cliffs, New Jersey, 1980.

Lambert, Douglas M., *The Distribution Channels Decision,* National Association of Accountants, New York, 1978.

Lewis, Edwin H., *Marketing Channels: Structure and Strategy,* McGraw Hill, New York, 1968.

Mallen, Bruce, *Principles of Marketing Channel Management*, Lexington Books, Massachusetts, 1977.

McCarthy, E. Jerome, *Basic Marketing: A Managerial Approach*, 5th Ed., Richard D. Irwin, Homewood, Ill., 1975.

McMillan, C. and S. Paulden, *Export Agents: A Complete Guide to their Selection and Control*, Gower Press, Epping, Essex: 1974.

Michman, Ronald, *Marketing Channels*, Grid Publishing, Columbus, Ohio, 1974.

———, and Stanley D. Sibley, *Marketing Channels and Strategies*, Grid Publishing, Columbus, Ohio, 1980.

Miners, N.J., *The Government and Politics of Hong Kong*, Hong Kong, 1975.

Moller, William G. and David L. Wileman, *Marketing Channels: A System Viewpoint*, Richard D. Irwin, Homewood, Ill., 1971.

Nie, Norman H., C. Hadlai Hull, Jean G. Jenkins, Karin Steinbrenner and Dale H. Bent, *Statistical Package for the Social Science*, 2nd Ed., McGraw Hill, New York, 1975.

Philpot, N. *Managing the Export Function*, British Institute of Management, London, 1975.

Rear, John, *New York: The Industrial Colony*, Oxford Press, London, 1975.

Rebushka, Alvin, *The Changing Face of Hong Kong*, Hoover Institute, Stanford University, 1973.

Robinson, R.D., *International Management*, Holt, Rinehart & Winston, New York, 1976.

Selltiz, Claire, Marie Jahoda, Morton Deutsch and Stuart Cook, *Research Methods in Social Relations*, Holt, Rinehart and Winston, Inc., New York, 1962.

Sethe, Prekash and Jagdish Seth, *Multinational Business Operations: Marketing Management*, Goodyear Publishing Co., 1973.

Stern, Louis W. (ed.), *Distribution Channels: Behavioral Dimensions*, Houghton Mifflin Co., 1969.

———, and Adel I. El-Ansary, *Marketing Channels*, Prentice-Hall, Inc., Englewood Cliffs, New Jersey, 1977.

Szczpanik, E.F., *The Economic Growth of Hong Kong*, Oxford Press, London, 1960.

Terpstra, Vern, *International Marketing*, The Dryden Press, Hinsdale, Ill., 1978.

Vernon, Raymond and Louis T. Wells, *Manager in the International Economy*, Prentice-Hall, Inc., Englewood Cliffs, New Jersey, 1976.

Walters, Glenn C., *Marketing Channels*, Goodyear Publishing Company, Santa Monica, California, 1977.

Weller, D., *Overseas Marketing and Selling*, Pitman, London, 1971.

Y.C. Yao, *Banking and Currency in Hong Kong*, Macmillan, London, 1974.

Articles and Periodicals

Bartels, Robert, "Marketing and Distribution Are Not Separate," *International Journal of Phusical Distribution*, 1976.

Beeth, G., "Distributors—Finding and Keeping the Good Ones," in *International Marketing Strategy*, H.B. Thorell, ed., Harmondsworth, Middx.: Penguin, 1973.

Bilkey, W.J. and G. Tesar, "The Export Behaviour of Smaller Sized Wisconsin Manufacturing Firms," *Journal of International Business Studies*, 7 (Spring), 1977.

Boyer, John, "The Widening of Hong Kong's Economic Base," *Proceedings of the Conference on Diversification of Hong Kong Industry*, Hong Kong, Hong Kong Management Association, 1978.

Buzzell, Robert D., Gale, Bradley T., and Sultan, Ralph G.M., "Market Share—A Key to Profitability," *Harvard Business Review*, January-February 1975.

Cook, Peter, "Focus on Hong Kong: Manufacturing Industry Gets a Bumpy Ride," *Far Eastern Economic Review*, Vol. 79, No. 11, March 1973.

Cunningham, M.T. and R.I. Spigel, "A Study in Successful Exporting," *British Journal of Marketing*, 5 (Spring), 1971.

_____, "International Marketing and Purchasing of Industrial Goods: Features of a European Research Project," *European Journal of Marketing,* 14 (5/6), 1980.

Etgar, M., "Channel Environment and Channel Leadership," *Journal of Marketing Research,* 14 (February), 1977.

Ford, I.D., and Rosson, P.J., "The Relationship Between Manufacturers and their Overseas Distributors," in *Export Management,* edited by M. Czinkota and G. Tesar, New York: Praeger, 1982.

Hakanson, H., and Wootz, B., "Supplier Selection in an International Environment: An Experimental Study," *Journal of Marketing Research,* February 1975, pp. 46-51.

Holloway, C., and King, W.R., "Evaluating Alternative Approaches to Strategic Planning," *Long Range Planning,* Vol. 12, August 1979.

Hunt, H.G., "Export Management in Medium Size Engineering Firms," *Journal of Management Studies,* February 1969.

_____, J.D. Froggatt and P.J. Hovell, "The Management of Export Marketing in Engineering Industries," *British Journal of Management,* Spring 1967.

Hsia, R., H. Ho and E. Lim, "The Structure and Growth of Hong Kong Economy," *Verbund Stiftung Deutsches Vbersee-Institut,* Germany, 1975.

Jao, Y.C., "Hong Kong's Export-Propelled Growth," *Intercon,* Hamburg, Gemany, September 1974.

Johanson, J. and F. Wiedersheim-Paul, "The Internationalization of the Firm—Four Swedish Cases," *Journal of Management Studies,* 12 (October), 1975.

Keegan, Warren, "A Conceptual Framework for Multinational Marketing," *Columbia Journal of World Business,* Vol. 7, November 1972.

Lambert, Douglas M., "The Distribution Channel Decisions: A Problem of Performance Measurement," *Management Accounting,* June 1978.

Lin, T.B. and Y.P. Ho, "Export Instabilities and Employment Fluctuation in Hong Kong's Manufacturing Industries," *Developing Economies,* Tokyo, June 1979.

Lusch, Robert F., Jon G. Udell and Gene R. Laczniak, "The Future of Marketing Strategy," *Business Horizons,* December 1976.

Mallen, Bruce E., "Functional Spinning-off: A Key to Anticipating Changes in Distribution Structure," *Journal of Marketing,* July 1973.

McDonald, A.L., Jr., "Do Your Distribution Channels Need Reshaping?" *Business Horizons,* Vol. 7, No. 2, 1964.

Michman, Ronald, "Channel Development and Innovation," *Marquette Business Review,* Spring 1971.

Paul, R.N., Donavan, N.B., and Taylor, J.W., "The Reality Gap in Strategic Planning," *Harvard Business Review,* May-June 1978.

Revzan, David A., "Evaluation of Channel Effectiveness," *Wholesaling in Marketing Organization,* John Wiley & Sons, New York, 1961.

Roering, K.J., E.A. Slusher and R.D. Schooler, "Commitment to Future Interactions in Marketing Transaction," *Journal of Applied Psychology,* 60, 3, 1975.

Rose, S. "The Poor Countries Turn From Buy-less to Sell-more," *Fortune,* Vol. 81, April 1970.

Ross, E., "Selection of the Overseas Distribution: An Empirical Framework," *International Journal of Physical Distribution,* Autumn 1972.

Schoeffler, Sydney, Buzzell, Robert D., and Heany, Donald F, "Impact of Strategic Planning on Profit Performance," *Harvard Business Review,* Vol. 52, March-April 1974.

Simmonds, K. and H. Smith, "The First Export Order: A Marketing Innovation," *British Journal of Marketing,* 2 (Summer), 1968.

Slijper, Martin, "Why We Must Wake Up to Distribution Now?" *Marketing (UK),* May 1978.

Stern, L.W. and T. Reve, "Distribution Channels as Political Economies: A Framework for Comparative Analysis," *Journal of Marketing,* 44 (Summer), 1980.

Stern, Robert H., "Hong Kong Lives to Trade, Trades to Live; It Can Be Rags to Riches or Rags to Rags," *Marketing News,* November 1977.

Sultan, Ralph, and Schoeffler, Sydney, "Profit Impact of Market Strategy," *Advertising Research Foundation Proceedings,* 18th Conference, New York: Advertising Research Foundation, 1972.

Sutu, H., "Industrialization in Hong Kong," *California Management Review,* Vol. 6, No. 1, Fall 1968.

Tookey, D.A., "Factors Associated with Success in Exporting," *Journal of Management Studies,* 1 (March), 1964.

_____, E. Lea and C.M.H. McDougall, *The Exporters: A Study of Organization, Staff and Training,* Ashridge, Berks: Ashridge Management College, 1967.

Weigand, Robert E., "The Marketing Organization, Channels and Firm Size," *Journal of Business,* Vol. 36, April 1963.

_____, "Fit Products and Channels to Your Markets," *Harvard Business Review,* February 1977.

Wiedersheim-Paul, F., H.D. Olson and L.S. Welch, "Pre-Export Activity: The First Step in Internationalization," *Journal of International Business Studies,* 8 (Spring/Summer), 1978.

Wind, Yoram, and Susan P. Douglas and H. Perlmutter, "Guidelines for Developing International Marketing Strategies," *Journal of Marketing,* Vol. 37, April 1973.

Other Sources

"Foreign Economic Trends: Hong Kong," American Consulate General, Hong Kong, various issues, 1975-1980.

Hang Seng Economic Quarterly, Hang Seng Bank, Hong Kong, April 1983.

Hong Kong, The Ernst & Whinney International Series, USA, 1980.

Hong Kong Annual Report, various years, Hong Kong, Government Printer, 1970-1983.

Hong Kong's Economy, Hong Kong, Trade Development Council, 1983.

Hong Kong into the '80s: Industrial Investment, Hong Kong, Government Printer, 1981.

Hong Kong Monthly Digest of Statistics, various issues, Hong Kong, Census and Statistics Department, 1975-1983.

Hong Kong Statistics, various years, Hong Kong, Government Printer, 1956-1983.

Hong Kong Review of Overseas Trade in 1979, Hong Kong, Census and Statistics Department, 1980.

Members' Directory of The Federation of Hong Kong Industries, Hong Kong, The Federation of Hong Kong Industries, 1978.

Index